Twayne's United States Authors Series

EDITOR OF THIS VOLUME

David J. Nordloh

Indiana University

Theodore Roosevelt

THEODORE ROOSEVELT

By ALOYSIUS A. NORTON

U.S. Merchant Marine Academy

TWAYNE PUBLISHERS
A DIVISION OF G. K. HALL & CO., BOSTON

Published in 1980 by Twayne Publishers,
A Division of G. K. Hall & Co.
All Rights Reserved

Printed on permanent/durable acid-free paper and bound
in the United States of America

First Printing

Frontispiece photo of Theodore Roosevelt © courtesy of the
Harvard College Library

Library of Congress Cataloging in Publication Data

Norton, Aloysius A.
Theodore Roosevelt.

(Twayne's United States authors series ; TUSAS 371)
Bibliography: p. 161–64
Includes index.
1. Roosevelt, Theodore, Pres. U. S., 1858–1919—
Literary art.
PS2734.R5Z79   907'.202'4   80–10713
ISBN 0–8057–7309–6

To
Samuel and Jane Leigh

Contents

About the Author

Aloysius A. Norton has degrees from the U.S. Military Academy, Columbia University, and the University of Madrid. His graduate studies investigated the relationships between literature and history. He has taught at West Point, Fairleigh-Dickinson University, Seton Hall University, Dickinson State College, Incarnate Word College, St. John's University, and is currently senior professor of English at the U.S. Merchant Marine Academy, Kings Point, N.Y. His previous publications include: co-author, *Literary Craftsmanship*; co-editor, *A Christian Approach to Western Literature*; author, *Huckleberry Finn: A Critical Analysis in Depth*; co-author, *The Language of the Merchant Marine in English*. He regularly writes reviews for *Choice*.

Preface

Theodore Roosevelt (1858–1919), the twenty-fifth President of the United States, devoted his entire life to politics, beginning his career at the lowest level of elective office in the New York State legislature and moving through various levels of appointments and elections to the presidency. Although in the average person's mind Roosevelt is usually recalled in Rough Rider gear ready to charge up San Juan Hill, Roosevelt was much more than a daring officer; and he never did charge up San Juan Hill. For more serious students of history, Roosevelt would very likely come first to mind as a reformer in politics. Those most familiar with his biographies will know that he pursued careers as a rancher, a conservationist, a big-game hunter, an explorer, and a writer of history, biography, and journalism. His intellectual interests, fueled by his voracious reading, ranged through all topics. Actually, his experiences in so many fields constitute an embodiment of the thought and interests of his time. He serves as a bridge between the thought and activity of the nineteenth and twentieth centuries.

What makes a study of Theodore Roosevelt even more compelling is that he produced over fifty books. Hundreds and probably even thousands of essays and books have been written about Roosevelt's various activities; these studies include not only his politics but also his multifarious interests, almost prodigious in diversity. However, except for an occasional essay or book review, no serious attempt has yet been made to examine the literary works of this man. A careful examination of bibliographies reveals no full-length volume that treats of Roosevelt solely as an author. Many of his books have never been out of print; some are reissued time and again. Since a constant and, in recent years, a growing interest in his publications persists, it seems appropriate to look at his work carefully: Roosevelt's serious efforts as an author should be remembered and appreciated as much as his political achievements. To do the many things which Roosevelt accomplished in his lifetime took tremendous physical stamina and courage; but there was also a great mind, just as productive, always at work within him. The purpose of this book is to examine the literary life of Theodore Roosevelt, to describe the contents of his works briefly, then to make a critical evaluation of these works, notably those in the National Edition, and finally to offer some appraisal of his place in literature.

It is fair to say what this book does not do. It does not attempt to analyze Roosevelt's political life or his reform programs. Such analyses are amply available elsewhere because almost every book written about Roosevelt has concentrated upon his presidential years or his social thinking. I am attempting to see Theodore Roosevelt as an author, giving attention to the literary aspects of his writings.

ALOYSIUS A. NORTON

United States Merchant Marine Academy
Kings Point, New York

Acknowledgments

I wish to acknowledge the generosity of the Theodore Roosevelt Association in permitting me to use the papers and published works of Theodore Roosevelt, the Harvard University Press for the use of the Morison edition of *The Letters of Theodore Roosevelt,* and Charles Scribner's Sons for quotations from the National Edition of *The Works of Theodore Roosevelt.* Also, I wish to express my thanks to Pauline Matthew and Professor A. Heimert of Harvard University for obtaining for me an appointment as Honorary Research Associate from the Harvard Corporation, and to Wallace Finley Dailey, Curator of the Theodore Roosevelt Collection. I wish to express my appreciation to John Gable, Executive Director of the Theodore Roosevelt Association, for many great favors. My colleague Lt. Cdr. Richard C. Bardot has been of indispensable assistance in reading my manuscript. Harold Lasher kindly typed the manuscript for me. Without the encouragement of Dr. Sidney Forman of Teachers College at Columbia University I might never have started this study.

To the staffs of the United States Merchant Marine Academy Library and the Great Neck Public Library I owe special thanks.

Chronology

1858   Born on October 27 at 28 East 20th Street, New York City, to Theodore and Martha Bulloch Roosevelt.

1880   Graduates from Harvard College; marries Alice Hathaway Lee.

1881   Elected to New York State Assembly.

1882   *The Naval War of 1812.*

1884   Mother and wife die on February 14; moves to his ranch in North Dakota.

1885   *Hunting Trips of a Ranchman.*

1886   Defeated in election for Mayor of New York City; marries Edith Kermit Carow.

1887   *Thomas Hart Benton.*

1888   *Gouverneur Morris; Ranch Life and the Hunting Trail.*

1889   Appointed to U.S. Civil Service Commission; *The Winning of the West,* Volumes I and II.

1891   *New York.*

1893   *The Wilderness Hunter.*

1894   *The Winning of the West,* Volume III.

1895   Assumes office as member of New York City Police Commission; *Hero Tales from American History,* with Henry Cabot Lodge.

1896   *The Winning of the West,* Volume IV.

1897   Appointed Assistant Secretary of Navy; *American Ideals and Other Essays Social and Political.*

1898   Commissioned as lieutenant colonel in First U.S. Volunteer Cavalry Regiment, known as the Rough Riders.

1899   Inaugurated as Governor of New York; *The Rough Riders.*

1900   *Oliver Cromwell; The Strenuous Life.*

1901   Inaugurated as Vice-President of the United States on March 4; sworn in as President on September 14 following death of President McKinley.

1904   Elected president for four more years.
1905   *Outdoor Pastimes of an American Hunter.*
1909   Hunting safari in Africa.
1910   *African Game Trails*; tour of Europe; contributing editor, *Outlook.*
1912   Defeated in election for president as candidate of Progressive party.
1913   *Theodore Roosevelt: An Autobiography*; travels in South America.
1914   *Through the Brazilian Wilderness.*
1915   *America and the World War.*
1916   *A Book-Lover's Holidays in the Open; Fear God and Take Your Own Part.*
1917   *The Foes of Our Own Household.*
1918   *The Great Adventure.*
1919   Dies at Sagamore Hill on January 6; *Theodore Roosevelt's Letters to His Children.*

CHAPTER 1

The Literary Life of Theodore Roosevelt

I *Youth*

THEODORE Roosevelt was born of Theodore Roosevelt, Sr., and Martha Bulloch Roosevelt on October 27, 1858, in New York City. He was descended of Dutch and Irish stock on his father's side, and of French Huguenot and Scots blood from his mother's family.[1] His mother was in every sense a Southern belle from Georgia, accustomed to life among slaves and fierce in her support of the South up to the outbreak of the Civil War. Even during the tumultuous antislavery demonstrations in New York City she dared to hang a Dixie banner outside her bedroom window at 33 East 20th Street.[2] But though she was a strong-willed woman, it cannot be said that Martha Roosevelt had as great a shaping influence on Theodore Roosevelt as his father did.

Theodore Roosevelt, Sr., inherited some money, made a moderate success in glass manufacturing, and then moved into banking. He was a remarkable man of kindly disposition, well known as a generous benefactor of the poor and unfortunate in New York. The older Roosevelt also had the most careful concern for each of his children, especially for his oldest daughter, who suffered from a spinal ailment, and for Theodore, who suffered from severe asthma. His sympathy for his daughter made him interested in other children similarly afflicted. Out of this concern was founded, with the help of Howard Potter and James M. Brown, the New York Orthopedic Hospital.[3]

Theodore Roosevelt was most deeply formed by the generous characteristics and influence of his father. When Theodore suffered a severe asthma attack, his father would bundle him up and drive his horse-drawn carriage at great speed through the streets of New York. No other treatment seemed to offer young Theodore any relief. His health was always frail in his younger years and really did not improve significantly until his later, long residence in North Dakota. His limited physical strength shaped him in the direction of strong mental concentration and particular interests.

Theodore Roosevelt, Sr., had attended the self-government school of John MacMullen, which was like that of Bronson Alcott's Temple School in Boston of about 1834. The early education of Theodore and the other Roosevelt children was unquestionably founded on the same liberal principles, with emphasis on individuality. Subordinations of self, honesty, and directness were to eliminate false pretentions and vanity.[4] Theodore was for a time enrolled in the MacMullen school; however, most of his education took place at home because of his poor health, his Aunt Anna being the principal tutor. Part of his schooling and remedy for his asthma included a trip to Europe with the family when he was ten. His diary entry of November 12, 1869, fairly well sums up his response to the trip abroad: "We have been half the time we are to stay abroad! hip! hurrah!"[5] By the time he made a second family trip to Europe, with a detour to Egypt, he was a dedicated student of nature; his diary of the period November 1872 to July 1873 resembles a technical ornithological text. His *Autobiography* explains that his interest in natural history began with his seeing a dead seal in a New York market. He measured the seal and began to write his first natural history. Apparently he managed to get the seal's skull and thus started, with two of his cousins, the "Roosevelt Museum of Natural History." The books of Thomas Mayne Reid, the British adventurer-novelist, provided his main inspiration. The museum was later considerably enlarged with specimens from the Nile collected during the trip there. He was also fortunate in having the support of his father, a trustee of the American Museum of Natural History, who gave him books on natural history by J. G. Wood, an English popularizer of this interest; his father also permitted him to take lessons in taxidermy. Despite his success in recording detailed observations, it was not until he received his first gun that he realized how poor his eyesight was. Writing of his first pair of glasses, he commented, "I had no idea how beautiful the world was until I got those spectacles."[6] Roosevelt wore glasses for the remainder of his life.

By the time he was fourteen, Theodore had acquired the habit of constant and wide-ranging reading. He began his lifelong interest in Scandinavian literature by reading Henry Wadsworth Longfellow's poem "The Saga of Olaf." In addition, he read dime novels, a magazine called *Our Young Folks,* Louise Ouida's *Under Two Flags,* novels by James Ballantyne and Frederick Marryat, and even stories for girls, such as *Pussy Willow, A Summer in Leslie Goldthwaite's Life,* and *An Old-Fashioned Girl.* He was also familiar with the evolutionary theories of Charles Darwin, especially as popularized by the philosopher Herbert Spencer and the American zoologist Spencer Fullerton Baird; in a letter of September 21, 1873, from Dresden, Germany, where he spent the summer learning German, he traced a Darwinian evolutionary process in reverse, he himself in four stages becoming a stork; his cousin Elliot, a bull; and cousin Johnny, a monkey. Roosevelt was fond of putting illustrations in letters throughout his life, and they are genuinely amusing. While in Dresden, the young Roosevelt began his interest in the *Nibelungenlied* and German poetry, which he loved as much as English poetry.

Upon his return to America he began his long stays at Oyster Bay, the summer home of the Roosevelts, as his father had before him. This Long Island, New York, location provided young Theodore a most suitable setting for his ornithological studies. With the tutorial assistance of Arthur Cutler, founder of the Cutler School of New York, Roosevelt was accepted at Harvard University for the study of natural history in the fall of 1876.

II   *Education, Formal and Otherwise*

Harvard University itself had little effect upon Theodore Roosevelt; he was sure that it did him some good, as he wrote in his *Autobiography,* "but only in the general effect, for there was very little in my actual studies which helped me in after-life." [7] He kept diaries during his four years at Cambridge, which included, of course, entries while at home or on vacation. These unpublished diaries reveal much of Roosevelt's relationship with his family, but especially with his father, the dearest of men to him. In the natural course of events it might have been very difficult for young Roosevelt to loosen the ties to his father; but his father died during his sophomore year at Harvard. It was a traumatic blow to Theodore, perhaps even more dif-

ficult for him to handle than anything else in his life. His diaries
reveal long months of introspection and mourning. Gradually
his interest in boxing, his studies, his ornithological hobbies,
and his religious beliefs eased the pain of loss. He came to
realize that he must rely only upon himself in life. Moreover,
the death of his father gave him a great sense of responsibility
for his family, and he matured remarkably.[8] Within five years he
was to publish his first important book, be elected to the New
York State Assembly, lose his mother and wife to death on the
same day, and retreat to a life of study and ranching in North
Dakota.

By the end of his junior year at Harvard in June 1879, he
was having a most pleasant time in his social life and with his
studies. His powers of concentration while reading became extraordinary. Once while he was reading a heavy book of
scientific German prose, his chair was bumped by a friend.
Roosevelt paid no attention. Finally, when the friend shouted
at him that his boots were being charred by the fire at his feet,
he moved. Additionally, he had developed the habit of throwing
himself completely into every activity. For example, while skat-
ing on Fresh Pond with classmate Richard Welling on a bitter
winter day, Roosevelt went endlessly round and round. Welling
had from boyhood accepted heavy weather as a challenge, but
this day was just too much for him. When Roosevelt shouted,
"Isn't this bully?" Welling could only wonder. He later commented, "It puzzled me how this youngster who had not my
health for he was asthmatic, and had not my muscle, for he would
be easy to throw over my shoulder, could want more of that winter gale." [9] This love of robust activity, together with his tremendous concentration in reading and study, marked Roosevelt's
character for the remainder of his life.

In January 1879 Roosevelt began to visit quite frequently the
Saltonstall family of Cambridge. He was quite taken with the
young ladies who visited there, especially with Alice Lee. During
his senior year his friendship with Alice became more serious,
and he began the earnest pursuit of her for his wife. It was not
an easy courtship for Roosevelt; he could not win her hand
despite their frequent meetings. His diary entry of Sunday, January 25, 1880, reveals his frustration: "I drove over to the Lees
determined to make an end to things at last. . . ." [10] His all-out
frontal assault was successful; Alice agreed to marry him.

During his vacation periods at Harvard it was usual for Roosevelt to go hunting, even to Maine, where the heavy weather required travel on snow shoes. On these trips he mixed freely with the common working men and became absolutely comfortable in their presence, as he had with the farmers and oystermen of Long Island. His affability and their acceptance of him shaped in Roosevelt the spirit of progressive politics that placed such great trust in ordinary men. This trait of being able to speak with all classes of men remained with Roosevelt all his life; it moved one observer to write: "He is always direct, always spontaneous, always concrete and specific, always interested and interesting. It is the style of the popular ballads, his favorite form of literature, plus a bit of his philosophy of action. There is no generalization without illustration; he speaks to the eye as well as to the ear, to Peter the Fisherman rather than to John the Divine, to the man of his hands who has built this nation." [11] After a church meeting in Maine, on September 14, 1879, while on vacation, Roosevelt wrote in his diary, "and I don't know a better or more intelligent race of men than these shrewd, plucky, honest Yankees—all of them hunters, lumbermen or small farmers." He acquired the same affection for the ranchers and hands of the Dakotas and for the men who ran the railroads. This instinctive fellowship supported his great faith in the ability of men to govern themselves, a theme that marks most of his political essays. Richard Welling reported him to say that the majority of plain people of the United States would make fewer mistakes in governing themselves than a minority smaller group trying to govern them.

Despite Roosevelt's disclaimer of Harvard's influence, this "most unHarvardlike man that ever came out of Harvard" [12] was surely formed and fixed in his character while an undergraduate. His remarkable and paradoxical personality never really changed after his years at Harvard: his sensibilities were both tender and brutal. Outwardly friendly and concerned, he kept his personal thoughts to himself; he had the greatest zest for living, yet was time and again afflicted with the sorrow of losing those he loved. He was a man who remained a boy all his life in his enthusiasm and appreciation of the whole, great world of men and nature.

On June 30, 1880, Theodore Roosevelt graduated twenty-first in a class of 158. He received a Phi Beta Kappa key but no honors. His intellectual interests, however, were not ending, but expanding. During his senior year he had become aware of the deficiencies of most accounts of the War of 1812 and decided to publish his own history of the naval operations of that war. He set to work on the project even before his graduation.

III Marriage and Political Beginnings

Shortly after returning to New York City in September 1880, Roosevelt entered Columbia University Law School, just prior to his marriage on October 27 to Alice Lee. He liked law school very much, reaching the point of arguing in moot court; but his interest in political activities and his disillusionment with the adversary method ended his law career after a little over one year. His entry for his diary of May 2, 1881, indicates that most of his spare time was spent in the Astor library working on his "Naval History."

On May 22 Theodore and Alice sailed on the *Celtic* for Europe to make the Grand Tour. The trip was important to his budding literary career because he spent some time with his Uncle James Dunwoodie Bulloch, who had superintended the building, equipping, and dispatching of the *Florida, Alabama,* and other Confederate cruisers at Liverpool, England. The old sea-captain provided him with many details of maneuvering the wind-driven sea vessels so important in his book.[13] While the couple was in Switzerland, Roosevelt continued to demonstrate his strenuous side by completing a two-day climb of the Matterhorn.

Upon their return to New York on October 2, 1881, on the *Brittanic*, the couple was met by both families. Roosevelt returned to law school on the sixth and also began work on the state primaries, vowing he was "going to kill our last year's legislator." On October 17 he wrote in his diary, "Am working fairly at my law, hard at politics, and hardest of all at my book which I expect to publish this winter." Then suddenly, on October 21, he was amazed to learn that he was nominated to the Assembly from the twenty-first district. His friends supported him, but his formal entry into active political life was bitterly opposed by his Uncle Jim, the nominal head of the Roosevelts, and cousins Al and Em. Today the country is accustomed to men of wealth and education in politics, but for Theodore Roosevelt to have entered New York City politics has always provoked a note of astonishment in historians because the level of political life in the Gilded Age was so low.[14] Actually, his decision came of his courage and early maturity, both derived from his experience with his father.

His diary entry of November 8, 1881, tells of his first political victory; he won a seat in the state assembly over William Straw by a majority of 1,501. But politics did not interfere with his work as an author; he sent his manuscript of *The Naval War of 1812* off to Putnam's on December 3, then went right to work on an aqueduct bill in the legislature. Although Roosevelt engrossed himself in his work, he had reservations about his future career; he wrote in a letter to Charles Grenfill Washburn right after the election, "But don't think I am going into politics after this year, for I am not." [15] And in a letter to his sister Anna he told of considering the purchase of a farm upstate: "Still, if I were perfectly certain that I would go on in politics and literature I should buy the farm without hesitation; but I consider the chances to be strongly favorable to my getting out of both—and if I intend to follow law or business I ought to stay in New York." [16] Nevertheless, the success of *The Naval War of 1812* must have helped him to make up his mind as to literature; and events in Albany provoked his moral courage to political action. His outspoken resistance to malicious legislation and his opposition to corrupt men in positions of committee leadership began his battle for Armageddon, which would, for him, take place in the world of politics; and writing would be his strong right arm.

During this period Roosevelt also maintained his close intellectual ties with Boston society. He and Alice stayed at the Somerset, where Percival Lowell gave a dinner for them. Robert Grant took him to St. Botolph's Club, where he first met Henry James and Cabot Lodge, General James Harrison Wilson, General Irvin McDowell, and Edward Everett Hale. James and Roosevelt later developed an appropriate contempt for one another; their natures were poles apart. Henry Cabot Lodge became Roosevelt's lifelong political adviser and close personal friend. The Civil War generals figured enormously in Roosevelt's life, for in later years the men of that war became a constant preoccupation in his speeches and writing. Admiring the men of the Civil War with a more deep-seated sense of awe and respect than he did his own Rough Riders, he always singled out the men of blue and cited them as examples of courage and idealism to his audiences. To him they represented in all its glory the Union, with all emphasis upon Union. One scholar of American civilization sees *The Strenuous Life*, Roosevelt's philosophy of living, as having its origins in the impact of the Civil War on his thinking.[17] Roosevelt's generation was the last markedly affected by the Civil War, and the impact figured significantly in his superpatriotism.

Roosevelt had reached a pinnacle of achievement by January 1884: his political career was going well; he had passed his examination for captain in the New York State National Guard; he owned a ranch in North Dakota; his *The Naval War of 1812* was already a text in colleges; and his wife was expecting their first child. Then, misfortune struck. He was called from Albany on February 13, 1884, because his child had been born, and arrived in New York City to find that his wife was terribly ill of Bright's disease and that his mother was dying of typhoid fever. Both died on February 14. His diary entry for that date is a large X and the words, "The light has gone out of my life."

On February 16 he wrote:

Alice Hathaway Lee. Born at Chestnut Hill, July 29th, 1861. I saw her first on Oct. 1878 [*sic*]; I wooed her for over a year before I won her; we were betrothed on Jan. 25th, 1880, and it was announced on Feb. 16th; on Oct. 27th of the same year we were married; we spent three years of happiness greater and more unalloyed than I have ever known fall to the lot of others; on Feb. 12th 1884 her baby was born, and on Feb. 14th she died in my arms, and my mother had died in the same house, on the same day, but a few hours previously. On Feb. 16th they were buried together in Greenwood. On Feb. 17th I christened the baby Alice Lee Roosevelt. For joy or for sorrow my life has now been lived out.

This quotation from his diary was altered somewhat in a small book he published through G. P. Putnam's Sons some time later for private distribution. *In Memory of My Darling Wife* commemorates the deaths of Alice Hathaway Roosevelt and Martha Bulloch Roosevelt, and contains a paragraph about his wife more tender than anything else he was to publish:

She was beautiful in face and form, and lovelier still in spirit; as a flower she grew, and as a fair young flower she died. Her life had been always in the sunshine; there had never come to her a single great sorrow; and none ever knew her who did not love and revere her for her bright, sunny temper and her saintly unselfishness. Fair, pure, and joyous as a maiden; loving, tender, and happy as a young wife; when she had just become a mother, when her life seemed to be just begun, and when the years seemed so bright before her— then, by a strange and terrible fate, death came to her.

And when my heart's dearest died, the light went from my life for ever.[18]

The obituary for his mother is much shorter: "With her duties done, and her joys and sorrows behind her—thus she died, in the fullness of her time." [19] The remainder of the book is a detailed account of the funeral service at the Fifth Avenue Presbyterian Church and the proceedings of the New York State Assembly Chamber, which adjourned for a weekend in sympathy for the young representative. Included also in its forty-five pages are reports Roosevelt copied from the *New York Evening Telegram*, the *New York Sun*, the *Savannah News*, the *New York Herald*, and the *New York Times*.

The voluminous clippings in the scrapbooks of the Theodore Roosevelt Collection at the Harvard College Library reveal that Roosevelt was back at work by February 20.[20] He truly buried himself in reform work: the *New York Times* of April 16, 1884, reported the passage of seven of his reform bills by the assembly on April 15. Soon after representing the Republicans of New York at the Chicago Convention in June 1884, he went to his two ranches in North Dakota, leaving his infant daughter, Alice, in the care of his sister Anna.

At first thought it might appear that grief over his wife's death and his mother's death drove Roosevelt to the West. Actually, the death of his father and the year-long grief over that death had prepared him for this later dual loss. His three terms in the assembly, which began when he was only twenty-four, had made him a national figure for, among other things, in 1883 he introduced into the New York State Assembly a bill which became the first State Civil Service Law in the United States. During his days at Harvard, Roosevelt had acquired a great liking for argument; he was a formidable adversary in any contentious discussion, likely to be sure of his facts, and tenacious to the bitter end in holding his position. He carried these traits with him into his political discussions and debates at Albany. As a result he made more political enemies than would an ordinary politician holding a position. He knew that he had moved very quickly into his political profession, but had not given himself time for anything but politics; he was tired of controversy and his interest in politics temporarily waned. In fact, the work of a mere state assemblyman was not a sufficient challenge to him. It was not the deaths in his family that caused him to move to North Dakota but rather a desire to reorder his whole life. He wrote in a letter of April 30, 1884, to Simon N. D. North, editor of the *Utica Morning Herald*, "Although not a very old man, I have yet lived a great deal of my life, and I have known sorrow too bitter and joy too keen to allow me to become either cast down or elated for more than a very brief period over any successes or defeat." [21] He also wrote to Carl Schurz, the great reformer, that the keenness of joy and the bitterness of sorrow were now behind him. He was tired and restless at the close of the assembly.

IV *Life in North Dakota*

Roosevelt arrived in the Bad Lands of North Dakota fully intending to write. The West of Frederic Remington's drawings and Owen Wister's stories was still the land of the buffalo-hunter, the soldier, and the cow-puncher. Roosevelt loved the life, and entered enthusiastically into his new career as rancher and hunter. His experiences provided him with materials for several books and for the most colorful chapters of his later *Autobiography*. The record of his growth as an author during this period appears in his extensive correspondence with Henry Cabot Lodge, himself an author. On March 8, 1885, Roosevelt congratulated Lodge on the first volume of the works of Alexander Hamilton, which Lodge was editing, and mentioned that his own manuscript for *Hunting Trips of a Ranchman* was in the hands of the printer. Roosevelt knew the illustrations would be excellent, but he had doubts about his own contribution; he considered writing to be "horribly hard work." [22] The great success of the *The Naval War of 1812* and then his new fame both in the United States and in England as the author of a book of western adventures prompted the publishers of the American Statesmen Series to commission him to write a life of Senator Thomas Hart Benton. Hard at work on the project, he found ideas readily in interpreting the senator's life, but he often lacked documentation for such information as the birthplace of President Benjamin Harrison. He appealed to Lodge for help, for he knew nothing of Benton after Benton left the Senate in 1850. The writing of a biography while hundreds of miles from a library or other resource demanded considerable inventiveness and ingenuity by the author, which he nonetheless completed in early August of 1886.

Although consideration of his health alone justified his move to North Dakota, other benefits followed. As for his health, Roosevelt's frailty while assemblyman prompted D. Willis James, the New York financier and philanthropist, to remark, "To think that the interests of our great city depend on that frail young man." [23] It was only after Roosevelt went to the Bad Lands of North Dakota and spent most of his time outdoors that he built the tremendous physique that ended his asthmatic problems. There is not any doubt that he was a most uncommon ranchman: he was not a good shot, not a good roper, or more than an average rider; he couldn't even cut down trees very well. But his love of ranch life and his unbounded enthusiasm for the task at hand combined with his ability to make friends quickly, and his great personal courage brought him the respect of all who knew him.

His residence in the West also served to strengthen his close literary friendship with Henry Cabot Lodge. He read Lodge's *Studies in History*, gave it to his cowboys to read, then delighted in telling Lodge that they thought early Puritanism must have been "darned rough on the kids!" [24] His correspondence with Lodge encouraged his literary production; he read magazines and argued in letters to the editors over such matters as the criticism of Lodge's book in the *Atlantic Monthly*. He also corresponded with such men as Lyman Copeland Draper, the historian of the early West. Draper influenced Roosevelt in the importance of accuracy and thoroughness, and he assisted Roosevelt in his search for unpublished manuscripts with which Roosevelt could begin *The Winning of the West*.

During his years as a ranchman Roosevelt managed to stay in the public eye. He wrote an article on the Civil Service for the *Princeton Review*. His work was reviewed both at home and in England. Furthermore, from time to time he did travel to New York to visit his child and thereby, by visits, maintained his political affiliations. Suddenly and most unexpectedly, he was

offered the nomination of the Republican party for the mayoralty
of New York City in October 1886. Out of party loyalty he accepted, ran, and was defeated; he knew he had not the slightest
chance from the outset. By this time he was accustomed to
writing, despite the press of campaigns and the responsibilities
of his political profession. In a letter to Frances Dana, a writer
of botanical studies for children, he tells of the *Century* printing
an article on "Machine Politics in New York City" and his being
solicited for six sporting articles by the same magazine.

Then, amid all this work, in another sudden move on the first
of November 1886, he wrote to a few close friends and relatives
that he was off to England to marry Miss Edith Carow, whom
he had known since childhood. They were married on December
2, 1886, with Cecil Spring Rice, a British diplomat, later ambassador to the United States, as best man.

V   *Civil Service Commissioner*

In the years between his marriage and his appointment to the
U.S. Civil Service Commission on May 13, 1889, Theodore Roosevelt devoted almost all of his time to writing. Barely thirty
years of age, he delighted people on both sides of the Atlantic;
the English lionized him as an adventurer-writer for his hunting
books written in North Dakota; certain people in the United
States knew that he was at work on a significant historical work.
His powers of memory were growing; he read more rapidly than
ever; he could write well under all circumstances. While in
Rome on his honeymoon, he finished the six articles on ranch
life for the *Century*, and in Venice he received his first copy of
Thomas Hart Benton, which he thought "a rather unequal book
—good in places and rough in others." [25] In his political thought
he had become distinctly progressive, shaped by his experience
on the range with the cow-punchers who taught him the meaning of justice. The same sympathies, he realized, were shared by
all Americans—mechanics, farmers, carpenters, and railway men.

Returning from the long honeymoon trip, Roosevelt spent most
of his time at Sagamore Hill, his home at Oyster Bay, Long
Island. Here he worked constantly at his next book, *The Winning of the West*. Occasionally he would turn out articles for
magazines or write book reviews. He also accepted a contract
for a book on Gouverneur Morris, the early American statesman,

which he completed during the summer of 1887. But *The Winning of the West* was his major concern. On April 23, 1888, Roosevelt wrote to Francis Parkman, the historian of the West whom he most admired, and described his intentions for the content of the *The Winning of the West*, which would emphasize the histories of Kentucky and Tennessee. He asked Parkman if he could dedicate the book to him, and Parkman consented.

Late in September 1888 James Brander Matthews, the noted professor of literature at Columbia University, asked Roosevelt to write a history of New York for the American Historic Town Series, edited by the British historian E. A. Freeman. (Henry Cabot Lodge wrote the history of Boston for the same series.) Roosevelt agreed, and immediately plunged into the work.

In the meantime, Roosevelt assumed the office of federal Civil Service Commissioner on May 13, 1889, upon appointment by President Benjamin Harrison, and moved to Washington, D.C. Roosevelt's acceptance of the post was wise politics: just into his thirties, he was not ready for high elective office such as that of senator or governor, but did need significant exposure. Despite his reservations about his political future in taking the appointment, he came to the commission precisely when it needed a strong man to give it direction and force. His stay in Washington brought him many new friends, and he was constantly stimulated and challenged by visitors to the capital. His six years in Washington provided him with more opportunities to write than might have been available under other circumstances of elective office or business.

In June 1889 *The Winning of the West* appeared in print and was pronounced "A Brilliant Work" by the *New York Tribune*.[26] Roosevelt's fullest gratitude went to Francis Parkman, who liked the book also. Roosevelt especially valued Parkman's praise, since he knew that Parkman, like himself, was not content with mere books of references but wanted work that demanded firsthand experience of the frontier.

Roosevelt read incessantly at this time. Hardly a periodical or newspaper escaped his notice. He was amazed that he did not know of the *Washington Star*, writing to Lodge, "I never even heard of it. If it is not better than the *Washington Post* it is vile indeed." [27] He read *Bedford's Magazine, Life,* the *Boston Herald,* the *Nation,* the *New York Sun* and *Advertiser,* the *New York Times,* and anything else brought to his attention.

Friends sent him articles, and, if sufficiently challenging, they would receive stiff replies—as in the instance of an item by James R. Gilmore, who had written an attack on *The Winning of the West*, accusing Roosevelt of not writing the book himself. Roosevelt dispatched him almost to critical oblivion in an exchange that appeared in the *New York Sun*.

Roosevelt wrote a considerable number of newspaper and magazine articles during this period: "Professionalism in Sports" appeared in the *North American Review*, "Religion and the Public Schools" in the *Boston Herald*. Considered an authority on naval warfare, he wrote reviews of Alfred Thayer Mahan's *The Influence of Sea Power Upon History* for the *Atlantic* in 1890, and of Mahan's *The Influence of Sea Power upon the French Revolution and Empire* for the *Atlantic* in 1893. He wrote a review of Parkman's *A Half Century of Conflict* for the *Independent*. His work with the Civil Service provided substance for many published articles, speeches, and letters. His name appeared as author in the *Atlantic Monthly*, the *Independent*, the *Forum*, the *Boston Herald*, the *Century*, the *Civil Service Reformer*, the *New York Tribune*, and a number of other publications.[28] By the time he left the Civil Service Commission in 1895, he had acquired a national reputation as an author. In answer to a query by Frederick William Kruse, Roosevelt, on April 6, 1891, answered as follows: "My books so far published are *The Winning of the West, Hunting Trips of a Ranchman, Ranch Life and the Hunting Trail, Essays on Practical Politics* (which contains some of my Albany experiences), the *Naval History of the War of 1812*, the *History of the City of New York*, the *Life of Gouverneur Morris*, and the *Life of Thomas Hart Benton*. Rather a formidable list, are they not? The best books among them are *The Winning of the West*, and the *Hunting Trips of a Ranchman*." [29]

James Brander Matthews aided greatly in his development as an author. Roosevelt made regular progress reports, or excuses, on his work with *New York* and the later volumes of *The Winning of the West*. His letters to Matthews demonstrate that he was very much aware of the literary scene in America. He considered Matthews, Edmund Stedman, and William Dean Howells, and the *Century*, *Scribner's*, and *Harper's* more important in determining New York's place in letters than clubs such as the Authors, the Players, or the Grolier. He confided in Matthews his initial displeasure with Rudyard Kipling but later modified his opinion considerably. Roosevelt resented Kipling's criticism of America. In addition, Roosevelt encouraged Matthews in efforts at revising the system of spelling, congratulating him on his article "As to American Spelling" in *Harper's Monthly* of July 1892. Roosevelt also shared this interest in correspondence with Professor Thomas Raynesford Lounsbury of Yale University. (As president, Roosevelt later attempted to alter the spelling system in government printing, but was thwarted by the Congress.[30])

The breadth of Roosevelt's interest and influence in American arts went beyond literature. His fundamental position demanded that what was American was as good as anything that Europe could produce and superior to anything that could be produced in Europe specifically for Americans. He remonstrated to Matthews regarding a bishop who got out a list of 150 books for American Sunday schools without one single American book on the list. Roosevelt thought the bishop himself should be taken for a text. He even went so far as to question the appropriateness of lions in front of the New York Public Library, very frankly proposing that they be replaced by the American bison. He despised all hints of colonialism and was outraged when the *Critic* in reviewing the *Life of Allston* spoke of Allston as the American Raphael, who should have remained in England to have a successful career as a painter. Roosevelt thought the article snobbish and un-American and sought to have the *Critic* change its policies. In the same vein he supported the work of Hamlin Garland; although he found some crudity and lack of cultivation in Garland's *Crumbling Idols*, he appreciated Garland's main thesis and purpose—to promote an American literature for Americans. Roosevelt wrote to Matthews: "We must strike out for ourselves; we must work according to our own ideas, and must free ourselves from the shackles of conventionality, before we can do anything." [31] In the same letter he expressed his dissatisfaction with the decadence of the *Yellow Book*, published in London, and remarked rather harshly on Henry James for his novels: "What a miserable little snob Henry James is. His polished, pointless, uninteresting stories about the upper social classes of England make one blush to think that he was once an American." [32] Roosevelt considered any expatriate something of a heretic, James being the worst sort.

In June 1893 Roosevelt finished and sent his *Wilderness Hunter* to Matthews, asking him to give special attention to the fourth chapter for its descriptions of natural life and also special attention "for the sake of allusions to Washington." [33] Roosevelt had access to George Washington's manuscript diaries and quoted extensively from them in the last chapter, "Hunting Lore." His whole purpose was to accentuate the first president's hunting interests. At the same time Roosevelt was hard at work on the third and fourth volumes of *The Winning of the West*. Writing was not simply an intellectual challenge: it offered the possibility of financial relief. He confided to his sister Anna on December 17, 1893, that his accounts had become tangled and that he was $2,500 behind his expenditures. Even his home at Sagamore Hill was in jeopardy. His only hope was through writing. "The trouble is," he wrote to Anna, "that my career has been a very pleasant, honorable and useful career for a man of means; but not the right career for a man without the means. If I can I shall hold this position another winter; about that time I shall publish my next two volumes of the *Winning of the West*; I am all at sea as to what I shall do afterwards." [34]

At the end of 1894 Roosevelt was offered the commissionership of street cleaning in New York City, a position he declined. In a letter to Carl Schurz he indicated that too many loose ends remained in his work in Washington. The New York offer no doubt did set him thinking. A letter to Jacob Riis on January 3, 1895, reveals his prolonged meditation on the appointment. Something more in his line might have been acceptable. So he went about his work, for the while, and collaborated with Henry Cabot Lodge in the production of *Hero Tales from American History*, whose purpose was to inspire patriotism without preaching. Lodge contributed twelve of the stories and Roosevelt, fourteen. Much of their personal pleasure in the writing came by their choosing an appropriate motto or quotation for each story. They had in mind the model of the works of Joseph Addison and Sir Walter Scott. When at a loss for a suitable quotation, Roosevelt or Lodge would create one and label it "Old Ballad," or "Old Play," or "Anonymous."

Roosevelt appealed to Governor Morton of New York on March 19, 1895, for the passage of a bill to remodel the public school system of New York. He then added a most peculiar request:

P.S. Private
In the very improbable event of a war with Spain I am going to beg
you with all my power to do me the greatest favor possible; get me a
position in New York's quota of the force sent out. Remember, I make
application now. I was three years captain in the 8th Regiment N.Y.
State militia, and I must have a commission in the force that goes to
Cuba! But of course there won't be any war.[35]

But the war which figured so significantly in Roosevelt's literary
and political career was still three years away.

VI *Police Commissioner*

By April 14, 1895, Roosevelt was no longer able to refuse a
persuasive offer to return to New York. At the urging of Lodge
and others, he accepted the position of police commissioner. He
wrote to Anna that he hated to leave Washington; the life was
good; and he doubted that he could do his literary work. Furthermore, he knew that he was going to an impossible assignment.
During his term as civil service commissioner under Harrison
and Cleveland the classified service had doubled in size. Again,
Roosevelt was the right man in the right job at the time. But it
was also time to move on.

From May 1895 to June 1897, while Roosevelt was police
commissioner, his writing output slowed down considerably, and
police work occupied most of his time. In almost every personal
letter of this period he remarked that he rarely left the office
before six or that he had more work on his hands than one could
imagine. He walked into a corrupt and demoralized situation
that demanded application of all of his energies. Week after week
he labored to get the police department under control. He
tramped the streets at night to make inspections; he presided at
departmental hearings; he made heroic efforts to enforce the
Sunday closing-laws for saloons, not only because they violated
the law, but also because they were sores of bribery and
influence on the police body. The beer-drinking working-class
people were offended by his campaign, yet he would not relent
until all were treated equally without bribes or favoritism. He
labored against prostitution, treating the men taken in the raids
exactly as the women. He sought to enlist worthy men into the

police force and promoted the deserving. His biggest setback came as he continued to enforce the ban on Sunday drinking in saloons. The law decreed that any man could take liquor with his meals. A magistrate was found who ruled that seventeen beers and one pretzel made a meal. The Sunday-closing ban was ended, but Roosevelt had curtailed the bribery of policemen.

More important than his routine work as Police Commissioner was his coming under the influence of Jacob Riis, a reporter and social reformer, author of *How the Other Half Lives* (1890). Riis took Roosevelt to the most neglected parts of the city, the tenement districts. The tenement people touched Roosevelt deeply: he saw the squalor of their lives and the impossibility of escape. Roosevelt always remembered Riis for awakening him so dramatically to the needs of the poor, even though as police commissioner he said, "I was still ignorant of the extent to which big men of wealth played a mischievous part in our industrial and social life, but I was well aware to the need of making ours in good faith both an economic and an industrial as well as a political democracy." [36] Wherever possible he used his power as police commissioner to better the life of the poor.

Besides Riis, Roosevelt knew many writers and artists in New York. Ingalls Kimball, the publisher, gave a luncheon for James Barrie, the English playwright, at the Players Club, and here Roosevelt met Hamlin Garland for the first time. Garland had begun to write for *Harper's Weekly*, and Roosevelt recognized a kindred spirit who loved the rugged life of the West as much as he did himself. Later Roosevelt wrote to Garland and invited him to witness the police machinery by making a tour of the precincts. At a hearing for dereliction of duty, Garland looked at the young fellow before them and whispered to Roosevelt, "Lemuel Barker from Willoughby Pastures!" [37] Roosevelt smiled as he recognized the plea for leniency in Garland's reference to the hero of Howells's *The Minister's Charge*, and let the offender off with a reprimand.

Roosevelt did find time to write some articles and reviews. He received $175 from *Scribner's* for a civil service article, "Six Years of Civil Service Reform." The *North American Review*, *Century, Bachelor of Arts*, the *Review of Reviews*, and *Forum* also published his articles. On December 23, 1895, he informed Cabot Lodge that he had finished the fourth volume of *The Winning of the West* and was pleased to say that the *Hero Tales*

were to be put into Braille by the *Century* people. No doubt he
would have done more, but the job of police commissioner
demanded too much from him. His task, he felt, was as heavy as
that of the President of the United States, particularly when he
was up against politicians, the press, and public apathy. He
acquired enemies because of his police reforms, for his outspoken
opinions on Venezuela's problems with Britain, and on Cuba.
The theme of Americanism permeated all his thinking. In writing
to Anna, he said that only a war with Spain could bring the
United States a proper navy.

During his hectic tour as police commissioner, Roosevelt
matured politically. He grew closer to Lodge's jingoism, fought
constantly with the entrenched conservative Thomas Collier
Platt and Platt's arm of his party, gave political addresses on all
occasions, and campaigned vigorously for McKinley in the West.
He saw the United States ready to become a world power of
righteousness.

VII   *Assistant Secretary of the Navy*

Roosevelt's appointment as Assistant Secretary of the Navy did
not come easily. He wrote to his sister Anna that he had no
ardent backers for the appointment from New York and that the
machine leaders hated him more than any other person in
politics. However, he had campaigned so vigorously for William
McKinley's election that he could not be denied the appointment
shepherded so carefully for him by Henry Cabot Lodge.

Because of his extensive knowledge of the history of the
United States Navy, his friendship with Captain Alfred Thayer
Mahan, and his own constant preoccupation with defenses,
Roosevelt came fully prepared for his appointment as Assistant
Secretary of the Navy. By April 22, 1897, he was already dis-
patching highly informed reports to President William McKinley
on the strength of the navy near Hawaii and the Mediterranean.
Despite the concerns of his new office, Roosevelt maintained his
interest in literary affairs. He wrote to Hamlin Garland to invite
him to dinner with Lodge and Brooks Adams. William Laird
Clowes had asked Roosevelt to write the portion of *The Royal
Navy* that covered the War of 1812, and Roosevelt had it nearly
completed shortly after becoming assistant secretary. He also
found time to debate the chief of the U.S. Biological Survey,

Clinton Hart Merriam, M.D., on the classification of species and to write on the subject for *Science*, and corresponded with Henry Fairfield Osborn on the subject. Merriam had the last word in the argument not long after by naming a new species of elk after Roosevelt—Cervus Roosevelti.[38] Soon after, the British editors of *The Encyclopedia of Sport* asked him for a series of articles on American game, which he completed. Both Longman and Macmillan also wanted him to write books. In June 1897 Roosevelt prepared *American Ideals*, a book of essays, for publication by Putnam's Sons. He always had the good sense to collect his previously published essays and reviews for publication in a special volume. In October he sent a copy off to William Allen White, the noted "grass-roots" editor of the Emporia, Kansas, *Gazette*.

Roosevelt had very serious intentions of continuing his story of the western expansion of the United States. He told Augustus Lowell of the Lowell Institute in Boston of his plans, explained to Frederic Remington that he intended to do for the plainsmen what he had done for the woodsmen, and even discussed specific months for completion of volumes five and six with George Haven Putnam, his publisher. However, in a letter to William Peterfield Trent, Roosevelt foretold, in effect, the fact that he would never write those portions of the *The Winning of the West*: "the press and bustle of city life and especially of the tendency to write 'timely' articles"[39] distracted him from the scholar's true pursuit.

Roosevelt's letters of this period of his life reveal that he had come into the fullness of his intellectual gifts. His wide reading and the cultivation of friendships with articulate men pushed him into prominence in American intellectual affairs. Jacob Riis, George Bird Grinnell, Frederic Remington, Carl Schurz, Alfred Thayer Mahan, and a host of other important people influenced him as he continued to be heard in a multitude of human activities. Nothing escaped his notice; if something might have, Lodge or someone else would call it to his attention. Roosevelt wrote to Stanley Waterloo to congratulate him on his work, especially *The Story of Ab*. He expressed his appreciation of a book by Arlo Bates which "dealt with Maeterlinck, Ibsen, Verlaine, Tolstoi, and the decadents generally."[40] He wished "Howells could be persuaded to read and profit"[41] by what Bates had written. To Owen Wister he wrote of Wister's *Lin McLean* in appreciation of the "broad humanity that comes when we deal with any men of strong and simple nature, with any kind of strenuous endeavor; and then it is a historic document for one phase of the life of endeavor in our race's history which is as evanescent as it is fascinating." [42] He told John William Fox that he was impressed by *The Kentuckians* and mentioned his admiration for James Lane Allen's *Choir Invisible*.

Beyond his appreciation of the intellectual life around him, Roosevelt had acquired a breadth of thinking suitable to those who would lead nations. He refused to limit his thought to particulars and responded broadly to matters of history and world affairs. Roosevelt could form opinions with confidence on the Roman Empire of the second century, the decline of France, the growth of Russia, the evils which afflicted Australia, and the destiny of the English-speaking peoples.[43] During this period he formed his strongest notions on race and the dangers of a falling population among Europeans and Americans. He considered the dangers to the world should there be a failure of will by the United States and the northern European nations to assume leadership. Such concern never left his attention.

His expertise in hunting skills continued to flourish while he was in Washington. He corresponded with the great Frederick Courteney Selous, African hunter. Roosevelt believed deeply in the contributions of big-game hunters and considered their work, done properly, often of more permanent value than scientific pamphlets on beetles or geology. He read every significant hunting book that he could find and even wrote to Rowland Ward, Ltd., in England concerning nine books not readily available in the United States, including Major Cumberland's *Sport on the Pamirs and Turkestand Steppes* and W. L. Distant's *A Naturalist in the Transvaal*. With George Grinnell he edited a third volume for the hunter-naturalist Boone and Crockett Club, *Trail and Camp Fire*, and did all that he could to strengthen and influence this conservation society, which he had helped to found.

Although Roosevelt was deeply involved in naval affairs, he expected to serve with the army should war with Spain come. He wrote to various offices in New York requesting that he be given a commission in the event of war, a war Roosevelt was certain would come. In a famous telegram to Admiral Dewey he gave specific directions to contain the Spanish squadron in the event of conflict. This action made it possible for Dewey to trap the

Spanish fleet in Manila Bay. On March 25, 1898, Roosevelt sent
a letter to John Davis Long, Secretary of the Navy, urging him
to give immediate attention to Professor Langley's flying machine
and to appoint "two officers of scientific attainments and practical ability, who in conjunction with two officers appointed by
the Secretary of War, shall meet and examine into the flying
machine, to inform us whether or not they think it could be
duplicated on a large scale, to make recommendations as to its
practicability and prepare estimates as to the cost." [44]

By now Roosevelt knew the country was ready for a war. He
referred to himself as "Jingo." [45] Fearing nothing except being
left out of the coming war, he made it plain in letters to various
authorities that he didn't want to be stuck at a desk. If anything,
he wanted to raise a regiment.

VIII *The Rough Rider*

After the destruction of the *Maine* in February 1898, Roosevelt
knew that war was imminent. He could not remain in his job in
Washington; he felt a responsibility for the drift toward war.
When the *New York Sun* published an editorial suggesting that
he stay on at the Navy Department, Roosevelt wrote a long letter
to Paul Dana and gave his reasons for wanting to serve in the
army. He said that he recognized the shift from civilian to
military leadership in time of war; also, he did not "expect any
military glory out of this Cuban war," [46] but merely wanted to
bear his share of the burden for a war he had been urging for two
years. His family was provided for; he had no reason to stay in
Washington. On April 25, 1898, the day that Congress declared
war, he was offered a colonelcy in a regiment of mounted riflemen to be raised in the Rocky Mountain states. Roosevelt preferred to be second in command, and was then appointed a
lieutenant colonel in the First U.S. Volunteer Cavalry, later
known as the Rough Riders. He sent a terse telegram to Brooks
Brothers clothiers on May 2nd: "Ordinary cavalry lieutenant
colonel's uniform in blue Cravenette." [47] On May 6 he resigned
his position as Assistant Secretary of the Navy.

The generation of sons whose fathers had fought the Civil
War now had their own war to fight; unfortunately they were
ill-prepared and had to move with shortages and confusion.
Roosevelt and Leonard Wood, an army surgeon, yet a colonel in

command, organized the regiment in a flurry of correspondence. They enlisted cowboys, Indians, Mexicans, Ivy League men, athletes, socialites, and lumbermen. Men were turned away in the hundreds. Roosevelt was proud to telegraph to Lincoln Steffens that men from the Knickerbocker and Somerset clubs and Harvard and Yale men would go as "troopers, to be exactly on a level with the cowboys." [48] Under persuasion, he even took the son of the Librarian of Congress and the son of the Chief of the Bureau of Navigation. No more wondrous military unit was ever formed in the United States. Few suffered such terrible wounds and sickness.

The author-businessman side of Roosevelt kept his wits about him, for on May 21 he wrote from San Antonio, Texas, to Robert Bridges of *Scribner's* that he was prepared to write the story of his military experiences if they would appear first in popular form in magazines and then as a book. Shortly after, he wrote directly to President McKinley, informing him that the rank and file of the regiment were better than any other, that remarkable progress had been achieved, and that they were ready for combat in Cuba with the very first troops. Just to be sure that Washington knew of his readiness, on the same day he sent a similar but longer letter to Henry Cabot Lodge and closed by asking Lodge to transmit his respects to the members of the Senate Committee on Foreign Affairs. Everything seemed so real and so unreal.

Roosevelt had told Paul Dana that he did not expect any military glory out of this Cuban war; and when the Rough Riders were moved to Tampa from San Antonio, he wrote to his sister Corinne, "I don't suppose there is much glory ahead." [49] But should there be, Roosevelt would not miss it. His determination surfaced in the great confusion of embarkation in Florida; he moved his men on empty coal cars from Tampa and literally seized a transport, the *Yucatan*, for passage with the invasion force. An entourage of foreign observers joined them in Cuba. The newspaper war had begun with its host of illustrators and reporters. Roosevelt was the darling of them all: Frederic Remington, Casper Whitney, Stephen Bonsal, Edward Marshall, John William Fox, Richard Harding Davis, Sylvester Scovel, James Hare, and Stephen Crane. Roosevelt spared Corinne none of the gruesome details: one man was killed by a bullet as he stood beside him; a bullet went through a tree and filled his eyes with bark; he had no rifle, so he took one from a wounded man and led another charge; the vultures plucked out the eyes of the dead and tore their faces and wounds; land crabs as big as rabbits "slowly gathered in gruesome rings around the fallen." [50]

Roosevelt was almost frantic by July 3. In a letter to Lodge he asked for more men, deplored the antiquated equipment which the troops used, complained about the leadership of the generals, and was amazed that after three days at the extreme front of the firing line he had not been killed. He slept in his clothes on the ground and drank putrid water. In the battle for the hills of San Juan, Roosevelt led not only his own volunteer troops, but the confused and leaderless remnants of the regular Third, Sixth, and Tenth, and the black troops of the Ninth Regiment. He led these troops up Kettle Hill and not San Juan Hill, as is popularly supposed. On July 17 Santiago surrendered. Only half of the 600 troops with whom he had landed were fit for duty. The heroism of the Rough Riders cannot be exaggerated, particularly the valor of the wounded who crawled and limped along on the assault. By July 23 Roosevelt wrote to the Secretary of War to boast of his troops as superior to any presently in the United States, including the regulars, and offered to invade Puerto Rico. Secretary Alger wrote what amounted to a severe reprimand in reply, warning Roosevelt of invidious comparisons. In less than a week Roosevelt had already received his first offer of nomination for the office of Governor of New York from John Lewis Childs, a Republican of Nassau County. However, Roosevelt had problems of more immediate concern. His troops suffered miserably from the fever on the island. Tired of delays, Roosevelt in most unmilitary fashion circulated a petition requesting that the army be moved out of Cuba to avoid the ravages of malaria and yellow fever. It was signed by three major generals, four brigadier generals, and one Colonel Roosevelt. The army was out of Cuba by August 14.

IX *Governor of New York*

Theodore Roosevelt returned with his Rough Riders from Cuba on board the transport *Miami* and landed at Montauk, Long Island. His only severe disappointment came of his not receiving the Congressional Medal of Honor, for which he had been recommended. For several months he waged a campaign of correspondence to force the army to cooperate in his receiving the medal. He had to be satisfied with the nomination by the New York

Republicans for the Governorship, promoted largely by Lemuel Ely Quigg, Republican editor and politician. Roosevelt waged an aggressive campaign and was elected. His heaviest opposition came from the antiwar and antiexpansionist people of his own party, mugwumps such as Carl Schurz, Edwin Lawrence Godkin, and Charles Henry Parkhurst. At this time Rudyard Kipling sent Roosevelt an advance copy of "The White Man's Burden," a poem pointing up the obligations of the United States toward Cuba and the Philippines. Roosevelt thought the poem "rather poor poetry, but good sense from the expansion viewpoint." [51] The first installment of his *The Rough Riders* was published by *Scribner's* in January 1899, the same month that he took office as Governor of New York. Once again Roosevelt continued his preference for publishing his work first in magazine serials and then as a book. On February 7 he signed the contract for the book with Robert Bridges, assistant editor of *Scribner's Magazine,* and indicated that he wished an appendix to include the letters of recommendation written in his behalf for the Medal of Honor, which he never received. Bridges complied.

In his other correspondence of this period, Roosevelt wrote to General Charles King on duty in the Philippines, encouraging him to keep copious notes and to publish a book of the campaign in the Philippines. Roosevelt expressed a desire to write a complete account of the Santiago campaign, but knew that he did not have the time while in politics. In thanking George Otto Trevelyan, the English historian, for a copy of *The American Revolution* (1899), Roosevelt pointed out that Trevelyan was "one of the few blessed exceptions to the rule that the readable historian is not truthful." [52] Roosevelt encouraged any number of authors in their work yet never hesitated to indicate any shortcoming. In a letter to George Francis Robert Henderson of the British army, Roosevelt complimented him on his *Stonewall Jackson and the American Civil War,* then stated that Lord Wolsey's work on the Civil War, in contrast, had no particular value. He went on to say that he objected to a footnote on *Uncle Tom's Cabin* included in Henderson's book, and added that his own revulsion toward slavery came from the fact that "the large class of mulatto slaves were practically sold into slavery by their own fathers." [53] Roosevelt knew of an instance of a white brother selling his half sisters.

In early August 1899 Caspar Whitney asked Roosevelt if he

would be interested in becoming editor of *Harper's Weekly*. Roosevelt knew that he could not be an editor while governor, but he did look forward to the day when he would leave politics and do "first-rate work in just such a position as editor of the *Weekly*." [54] He realized the perils of authorship in anticipating that some of the things he had said in his recently completed *Oliver Cromwell* would not help him politically. He was still getting letters from outraged people twelve years after the publication of *Gouverneur Morris*, in which he called Thomas Paine a "filthy little atheist," an appellation Roosevelt stoutly maintained as true.[55] He also took his chances by publishing *The Strenuous Life*, in which he gave his philosophy of life, sure to alienate a significant portion of the population. Very few politicians can afford the risks of putting their strongest opinions into print; Roosevelt ignored the ridicule and laughter and continued to publish. By October 1899 he was able to spare $2,000 from his literary earnings for Douglas Robinson, his brother-in-law, to invest for him.

In 1899 G. P. Putnam's Sons issued Roosevelt's *Big Game Hunting*; this book was merely a combined volume which included *Hunting Trips of a Ranchman* and *The Wilderness Hunter*. In the meantime, Roosevelt was finishing his biography of Oliver Cromwell for *Scribner's*; it was published in serial form from January to June 1900 and then issued as a book. In a letter to Robert Bridges, Roosevelt declared that the work was not a rehash of anyone else's work and not simply a series of annals. He also cautioned Bridges not to use too many pictures in the book version because they would detract from the dignity of the work and suggest that it was not serious history. The book was extensively reviewed in the United States and England.

X *Vice-President*

Roosevelt's work as governor taxed him only insofar as he had to work with the leader of the Republican party machine, Thomas Collier Platt. Roosevelt acknowledged that he did not have great power in party affairs; he was constantly in disagreement over matters such as selections for appointed offices. He believed luck played a large role in his election and did not think that he would be reelected governor.

Roosevelt was more correct than he realized. He was not

continued as governor because Senator Platt wanted him out of New York State. The corporations had become infuriated over Roosevelt's appointments and his refusal to bend to their wills. He tells the story in his *Autobiography* of being pushed for vice-president against his own wishes. However, once again party loyalty manipulated him into accepting the nomination.

Despite the heavy demands of the campaign of 1900, Roosevelt managed to read on his travels. He particularly enjoyed the novels of Henry Sienkiewicz, excepting *Quo Vadis*. He took great interest in the Boer War and wrote regularly to Frederick Courteney Selous, the African Hunter, for information. Roosevelt was convinced of the superiority of the English in the interests of civilization. His political thinking had become global; in his correspondence he wrote of China, of Russia, of a canal through Central America. He corresponded with a great many writers and newspaper editors both in the United States and in England. To Peter Finley Dunne, Roosevelt wrote, "I regret to state that my family and intimate friends are delighted with your review of my book." [56] Dunne had poked fun at Roosevelt for his *Rough Riders* in his Dooley Column, and Roosevelt enjoyed it immensely. He also took Dunne seriously and invited him to his home in Oyster Bay.

Roosevelt departed on a five-week hunting trip in the West soon after the successful election campaign. He was eager to hunt cougar with the hounds of John B. Goff. This trip furnished him with material for a hunting article which appeared in *Scribner's* in October, after he took the oath of office as vice-president. It later formed the leading essay in *Outdoor Pastimes of an American Hunter*, published in 1905, when he was president. Roosevelt killed twelve cougars on this trip; on four occasions he dismounted and ended them with his knife—a remarkable action for a Vice-President of the United States. He had all twelve mountain lions mounted, and then distributed them to his friends.

A few days of work as vice-president convinced Roosevelt that his political career was about finished and that he had little chance to do very much. He wrote to James Lowndes, a Washington attorney, to John Proctor Clarke of New York, and to Alton Brooks Parker to assist him in earning his law degree. He referred to his year at Columbia and wanted to decide whether to try for the bar in Washington or in New York. New York seemed more practical for his future intentions. His usual occupation of author was somewhat thwarted by his new office. He deplored the possibility that his work would be published because he was vice-president, and even cautioned against such a practice. In a letter to William Henry Rideing of the *Youth's Companion*, Roosevelt spoke of an article, "The Essence of Heroism," which had been delayed in appearing. Roosevelt wrote to Associate Editor Rideing, "You of course remember that it was explicitly understood that it should appear prior to my being inaugurated as Vice-President. Frankly I should not have written the article 'The Essence of Heroism' if I had not supposed you would have published it at once." [57] (Roosevelt had exactly the same reserve in the showing of his hunting trophies, and was similarly disturbed with C. G. Guther's Sons, taxidermists, for admitting the press as visitors to his collection of mountain lions.) He wanted to avoid any advantage that might fall to him because of his new office. However, he could make speeches and give lectures. All of these were amply covered by the press and some were later collected as separate volumes. He did manage to place an article in *McClure's* which was later reprinted in *American Ideals* and titled "Reform through Social Life." He also did a small piece for *Christian Age* called "What the Bible Teaches."

Roosevelt's enormous correspondence with men of letters continued. In thanking Hamlin Garland for sending *Her Mountain Lover*, he wrote of kindred feelings that he shared with Garland for the outdoors. Owen Wister had called Roosevelt's attention to *The Octopus*, by Frank Norris; Roosevelt appreciated the ideas and power of Norris but thought "his overstatement was so utterly preposterous as to deprive his work of all value." [58] Roosevelt had met Augustus Saint-Gaudens on a train with Finley Peter Dunne and soon made a friend of the sculptor. Roosevelt had an absolute custom of entertaining at Oyster Bay anyone whose company he enjoyed. People from every area of accomplishment were invited to his home not merely for dinner, but for a two- or-three-day stay. Only the rich were singularly unattractive to Roosevelt. He considered his own life a thousand times as happy as that of any of the very rich men whom he knew, and he realized that very few of them possessed the traits which would make them companionable to him.

Roosevelt continued during this period to read deeply in history. To Hugo Münsterberg of Harvard he wrote that he would greatly enjoy a position on a university graduate faculty and to be able to write history equal to that of Henry Charles Lea and John Fiske, although he did not aspire to equal Francis Parkman and John Lothrop Motley.

But suddenly Roosevelt did not have to be concerned about his future in either law or letters, for he succeeded to the presidency on September 14, 1901, when McKinley died of an assassin's bullet. There can be little doubt that his extensive knowledge of history and the global political situation prepared him for the leadership which would make the United States a significant world power.

XI *President*

At age forty-three Roosevelt moved into the White House with his wife, Edith; Alice, his first daughter; and the five children of his second marriage, Theodore, Kermit, Ethel, Archibald, and Quentin. With such a number of young, active people the White House became a site of constant activity and surprise.

Roosevelt did not write very much for publication while he was president. His various speeches, of course, were printed in newspapers and magazines. He had found the perfect pulpit for the propagation of his ideals of morality, the presidency; and he preached his doctrines to the people of the United States at every opportunity. He occasionally would forward an article for publication if he thought it within the bounds of decorum. In 1904 he sent an article titled "The Merit System of Government Appointments" to *Cosmopolitan*. *Forest and Stream* printed an article called "Wilderness Reserves," which later appeared in the regular publication of the Boone and Crockett Club. A speech called "The American Woman as a Mother" found its way into the *Ladies' Home Journal* for July 1905. Various hunting articles appeared, such as "A Colorado Bear Hunt," given to *Scribner's*; and "A Wolf Hunt in Oklahoma," rewritten from the 1897 version, was given to *Trail and Campfire*. The most unusual article was a review for *Outlook* of *The Children of the Night* by Edwin Arlington Robinson. Roosevelt encouraged Robinson in his career at every opportunity, and with this review rekindled an interest in Robinson's poetry. Later, Roosevelt provided Robinson with an income through a government job.

In 1906 Roosevelt began a regular series for the *Ladies' Home Journal* called "The President." These articles were directed at the families of America; topics ranged from race suicide to factory laws for women and children, and included sports, divorce, the definition of a gentleman, and Roosevelt's views on The Strenuous Life. In the same year of his presidency, when he wrote "The Man with the Muck-rake" for the April *Outlook*, "muckraking," with a different connotation, entered the American vocabulary.

In 1907 *Century* magazine paid him $1,000 for an article titled "The Ancient Irish Sagas." [59] This article surprised a considerable number of citizens in all walks of life who were unfamiliar with the president's scholarship and catholicity of interests. To his closest friends it was no surprise. *Metropolitan* published his report to Congress on Fur Seal Fisheries; *Sewanee Review* accepted "Robert E. Lee and the Nation," which, again, caused controversy among those in the North still fighting the Civil War. His continuing series in the *Ladies' Home Journal* included "Objections to Modern School Methods," and "Rules for the Conduct of Life." The *Women's Home Companion* printed "Where I Stand on Child Labor Reform," and *National Geographic Magazine* featured his address on Admiral Robert E. Peary's polar explorations.

During 1907 Roosevelt became embroiled in a significant nature controversy that raged for some time. Edward B. Clark interviewed Roosevelt on the matter of colorations in animals to protect them from marauders, then submitted the article to Roosevelt for corrections and additions. (His changes were so extensive that the article could really be attributed more to Roosevelt than to Clark.) In any event, the article, called "Roosevelt on the Nature Fakirs," appeared in *Everybody's* of June 1907, setting off a storm of argument. Roosevelt had attacked the work of W. S. Long, E. T. Seton, Jack London, and C. G. D. Roberts for misrepresenting the habits of wild animals. Roosevelt was infuriated by what he considered sentimental misinformation which found its way into school textbooks. John Burroughs, the famed naturalist, soon joined Roosevelt's allies. Articles and letters crisscrossed the United States, heightening the interest of young people in the creatures of forest and plain. [60] Roosevelt also wrote a nature article for *Scribner's* called "Small Country Neighbors." This article drew upon his nature notes of the Oyster Bay area of Long Island.

During his presidency translations of his works began to appear in Berlin, Barcelona, Warsaw, and Paris. Also, reprints of his earlier works aroused renewed interest. An autobiographical letter he wrote while in Albany in 1884 was printed in *Cosmopolitan* for November 1907, then reprinted in London and Paris. An article from *Murray's* magazine of September 1888 of autobiographical interest was also reprinted as "The T.R. of 20 Years Ago" in *Market World*.[61]

The last year of Roosevelt's presidency produced regular publication of his addresses in such magazines and journals as *Good Housekeeping* and *The Journal of Education*. Also, "In the Louisiana Canebrakes" was printed by *Scribner's* in January 1908 and later appeared in the collection *Outdoor Pastimes*. *Collier's* printed "Lincoln" in February; *The Home Magazine* issued an exchange of letters between Roosevelt and Julian Harris, son of the author of the Uncle Remus stories.[62]

Long before Roosevelt left the presidency, he knew the problems of being only fifty years of age with no immediate desire for further political office. He had a great interest in big game and prided himself on owning one of the most extensive big-game libraries in the world. He owned original works dated as early as the sixteenth century, and reproductions from the Middle Ages, including a copy of a book of the Emperor Maximilian, and the Duke of York's translation of Gaston Phoebus. Because he wanted to remove himself from American politics, Roosevelt began to plan a hunting trip to Africa while still president. In realistic fashion he wrote to Courteney Selous, Leigh S. J. Hunt, and John Henry Patterson as early as March 20, 1908. He gave a year to his preparations and followed the advice of the experts wherever possible. When he informed the Smithsonian Institution of his plan of landing at Mombasa and traversing British and German East Africa toward Uganda and the Nile, they eagerly enlisted his assistance in gathering specimens for the National Museum. To cover his personal expenses, Roosevelt made arrangements with Robert Bridges of *Scribner's* for reports of his travels. Although offered $100,000 by the publisher Robert J. Collier, Roosevelt accepted $50,000 from *Scribner's* because he did not believe that the writing would be worth $100,000.

In August 1908 Roosevelt received an invitation from the Chancellor of Oxford University to give the Romanes Lecture, founded in 1891 and offered annually by naturalists of great reputation. (He also would receive an honarary LL.D. at the conclusion of his African trip.) Similar invitations came from the Sorbonne and the University of Berlin. Roosevelt had retained some fluency in French and German, especially in reading, and at the time of these invitations had just finished the French translation of Guglielmo Ferrero's last volumes and *La Production, le Travail et le Problème Social dans Tous les Pays au Début du XXme Siècle* by Léon Ponsard. Roosevelt took serious interest in his status as an ex-president and struggled gamely to avoid any embarrassment to anyone, especially in the instance of being invited to visit the Kaiser. In much of his correspondence of August and September 1908 he remarked that he was acutely aware of his coming role as ex-president and private citizen. He asserted his wish to avoid mock honors and to go his own way. Although he received many other invitations pertaining to his forthcoming visit to Africa and then Europe, he settled upon Oxford, the Sorbonne, and Berlin. He finished work on his Romanes lecture and Sorbonne address in early November 1908 before the Congress was in session.

XII *Journeys through Africa and Europe*

In August 1908 Roosevelt told Lodge that he had made provisions for work after leaving the presidency. He arranged for an editorship with *Outlook* to write on social, political, or economic subjects. For $12,000 a year he would write monthly articles of from 1,000 to 5,000 words each. He had offers of more money but preferred *Outlook* because it came closest to his convictions. On March 6, 1909, no longer president, he published in *Outlook* his credo, "Why I believe in the kind of American journalism for which the *Outlook* stands." He had found the occupation he desired—journalist. He then began to produce, regularly, signed articles and editorials for the magazine.

On March 23, 1909, he sailed for his African adventure. Accompanying him were his son Kermit and the naturalists Edgar Alexander Mearns, Edmund Heller, and J. Alden Loring. By May 12, 1909, Roosevelt had finished his first African articles for *Scribner's* and told Bridges that three more of 7,000 or 8,000 words each would soon follow. He planned six more chapters within a month. In June he was able to tell Bridges that the first four promised chapters were on their way and that when the serial was finished and put into book form it should be titled *African Game Trails*, with the subtitle: *An Account of the African Wanderings of an American Hunter Naturalist.* *Scribner's* began printing the articles in October 1909.

What is most revealing, if not amazing, about Roosevelt on this safari is that he continued his intellectual life, just as he had on the trail in North Dakota and Montana when a young man. For reading he had approximately fifty books bound in pigskin by John T. Loomis of Washington. The Pigskin Library, as it was later called, contained such works as the *Chanson de Roland*; the *Nibelungenlied*; the Bible; novels of Thackeray, Dickens, Cooper, and Mark Twain; Dante's *Inferno*; and a number of the writings of the historian Thomas Babington Macaulay. Roosevelt had profound admiration for Macaulay; in a letter to George Otto Trevelyan from Mount Kenya, Roosevelt mentioned that his most worn volumes were those of Macaulay. On the other hand, he also told his historian friend Trevelyan in extravagant terms of his utter contempt for Thomas Carlyle and his histories. He also wrote to Cabot Lodge, saying he was seriously disturbed with Charles William Eliot's selection for the famous five-foot shelf of books. He could not understand how Eliot would leave out Cervantes and Montaigne and include Woolman's *Journal*, which he had never heard of. He felt a sense of outrage that Herodotus, Tacitus, and Thucydides had been left out, as had Aeschylus, Sophocles, Molière, and Calderón. He could hardly believe that the list included the *Aeneid* and left out Homer. Not many people would be so exercised over such matters while in the middle of Africa.

Even though Roosevelt and his son killed many animals on this expedition, their true purpose was to collect specimens. The various hunts which took them from Nairobi to the Uasin Gishu plateau and then to Njoro furnished more and more species. The count in British East Africa alone came to 550 large mammals, 3,379 small mammals, 2,784 birds, about 1,500 reptiles and batrachians, and 250 fish. The expedition gathered for the National Museum the most extensive collection of East African specimens ever assembled. Two hundred bearers were required just for the scientific needs of the safari. Roosevelt published a complete inventory in his book; many of his species are still in the Smithsonian.

Events on both sides of the Atlantic continued to touch

Roosevelt's life during his time in Africa. At the close of his safari, he met Mrs. Roosevelt and his daughter Ethel, and proceeded to Cairo. There he was immediately drawn into world
affairs, first with the English and Egypt, then over his proposed
visits to the Kaiser and the Pope. Andrew Carnegie tried to make
Roosevelt an ambassador of peace to the Kaiser; the Pope's office placed an unacceptable condition on his visit, that he not
visit the Methodist Mission. Roosevelt's public utterances of his
disdain for British rule in Egypt constituted only the beginning
of his notoriety.

Roosevelt delivered his address at the Sorbonne at the end
of April. He himself was unable to gauge the effect of his speech
on citizenship. It has been suggested that the French thought
his concepts naive. Roosevelt was by now firmly fixed into a
pattern of thoughts on "sound character, homely virtues, virility,
cynicism, sterility, and social efficiency. In any case the French
Republicans were delighted, the Royalists relieved, and the
Socialists as contemptuous as they had planned to be." [63]

Roosevelt spoke at the University of Berlin. This speech and
the Romanes lecture given at Oxford on June 7 were collected
together with his other speeches delivered while he was abroad
in 1910 and published as *African and European Addresses* the
same year. Many appeared in the *Outlook* from month to month.
Actually, Roosevelt made one detour from his originally planned
itinerary, obliging the Nobel Prize people by journeying to
Christiania, Norway, to give his "League of Peace" address and
to accept his award for ending the Russian-Japanese War while
president. His return voyage to the United States provided him
the time to finish the appendixes for the book version of
African Game Trails. One appendix developed the familiar tor-
rent of protest from Abbot H. Thayer and other naturalists on
the matter of protective coloring in birds and animals.

His arrival in New York filled the harbor and docksides with
welcomers in the thousands, among them young distant cousin
Franklin Delano Roosevelt. The welcome carried with it obligations for appearances and speeches. Despite Roosevelt's strong
efforts where appropriate to aid the Republican party, 1910 produced a series of defeats. Even in Roosevelt's home district his
own congressman was defeated. Roosevelt gradually lost faith
in President William Howard Taft, his successor, and worried
considerably over the future of progressive politics.

During his political preoccupations he still continued his support of writers. He wrote a letter of appreciation to Edwin Arlington Robinson, who had dedicated *The Town Down the River* to Roosevelt. One poem in the volume, "The Revealer," is about Roosevelt. Roosevelt wrote to Robinson, "I believe in you more than ever." [64] To Gouverneur Morris, another contemporary author, he wrote a letter of thanks for some books and asked him to visit Oyster Bay. He followed the work of Homer Lea, and read most of the first three volumes of James George Frazer's *Totemism and Exogamy*. His detailed analysis of a book from General Ian Hamilton on compulsory service in the British army permitted him to make comparisons with the American experience in Cuba. Recognition of Roosevelt's own writing came in his being elected vice-president of the American Historical Association in 1911 and president in 1912. (Previously, in 1898, he had been elected one of the original members of the National Institute of Arts and Letters; and when the American Academy of Arts and Letters was founded in 1904, he was one of the first fifteen elected to membership.)

Roosevelt's work for *Outlook* covered a wide range of topics. One essay, "Dante and the Bowery," praised Dante for his willingness to stigmatize the living evil of his own time in literature. However, most of Roosevelt's writing pertained to problems in society and education. He also wrote articles for the *Missionary, Review of the World,* and the *Literary Digest. National Geographic* published a lecture he had given called "Wild Man and Wild Beast in Africa." At the University of California he delivered the Earl Lectures and preached his favorite topic— political morality. The lectures appeared in book form as *Realizable Ideals.* Continuing his extensive correspondence, on October 1, 1911, he sent a letter of over 20,000 words to George Otto Trevelyan which is undoubtedly the most comprehensive and personal report of his European travels after the safari. It is in his correspondence that Roosevelt reveals the enormous breadth of his reading. For example, in one instance he wrote knowledgeably of the writings of Carmen Sylva on Romanian folk songs and the poetry of the Balkan Slavs; and in another letter he told how in meeting one of the heads of a college at Oxford, he conversed with him on the man's *Ghost Stories of an Antiquary,* the best ghost stories Roosevelt had ever read. In fact, there was hardly a writer whom he met at Oxford, includ-

ing Kenneth Grahame, Andrew Lang, and Charles Oman, whose
works he had not read. The detailed personal account of his visit
to England was assembled by Roosevelt in a letter to David
Gray almost as long as the one sent to Trevelyan. Roosevelt
mentioned that his best day had been the last, when he roamed
the Valley of the Itchen and New Forest with Edward Grey to
listen to English bird songs.

XIII *Bull Moose*

In October 1911 Roosevelt began to take very seriously the
rumors of action to nominate him again for president. In a letter
to William Allen White he tried to make plain that he wanted
no part of any movement to have himself nominated. Despite
his resistance and his complete understanding of the power of
Nelson Aldrich and Joseph G. Cannon and others behind Taft,
Roosevelt was gradually drawn into the campaign of 1912.
Various governors began to persuade him to commit himself to
candidacy as a Progressive Republican. His entry into the campaign put him at odds with Cabot Lodge, who was almost heart-
broken over the situation in which he found himself—loyal to
President Taft and fond of Roosevelt, his friend. Roosevelt as-
sured Lodge that nothing could alter their friendship. When
Roosevelt did not receive the nomination, he was convinced that
he had been cheated. He then formed the National Progressive
party—the Bull Moose party—and ran for president at the head
of the ticket. Even today no one fully understands his decision
to bolt his own party and assure the election of Woodrow Wilson.

In the midst of the campaign, an assassin shot Roosevelt in
the right side of his chest. His spectacle case had saved him
from the danger of no more serious a wound than a deep
laceration and a fractured rib. After a brief stay in the hospital,
Roosevelt finished the campaign, which Wilson won. Roosevelt
never really had expected to win a victory for his Bull Moose
party.

Roosevelt immediately resumed his interests away from politics. He informed the editor of the *Auk*, the journal of the
American Ornithologists' Union, in enormous detail that the
October issue had printed an offensive and untruthful attack
upon him and in favor of Thayer in the matter of protective

coloration. The editor apologized for his acceptance of Thayer's "dreadful paper" for publication.[65] As president of the American Historical Association, Roosevelt delivered one of his finest academic addresses, "History as Literature," on December 27, 1912. He then began work on his *Autobiography*, which was published serially by *Outlook* between February 22 and December 27, 1913. The various issues were syndicated throughout the country in newspapers. He also nurtured Franklin Delano Roosevelt in certain aspects of his political career, especially in his old office as Assistant Secretary of the Navy, and warned FDR to keep the fleet in the Pacific alert against Japanese attack: "It may come, and if it does it will come suddenly." [66]

XIV   *Journey through Brazil*

In October 1913 Roosevelt began a tour of South America. While in Brazil, he was offered the leadership of an exploratory mission of an unknown river. Despite the fact that while in Africa in 1909 he considered himself "an elderly man" and "an old man," he thought the exploration "a feat worth doing." [67] His son Kermit and the American naturalist George K. Cherrie were to accompany him, guided by Colonel Candido Mariano da Silva Rondon, a competent explorer for the Brazilian Telegraphic Commission. Roosevelt could not have known how dreadfully difficult the journey down the river would be. Repeatedly the party had to carry their canoes and supplies in portage along rapids, suffer with every form of insect, almost run out of food, and all but abandon themselves to despair. After forty-two days they emerged from the jungle, and out of the trip came the successful exploration of the Rio da Dúvida (known today as the Theodore Roosevelt River on maps of South America). Roosevelt published the story of his voyage in serial form in *Scribner's Magazine* the following April to November. The chapters appeared as a book called *Through the Brazilian Wilderness*. The extreme suffering and fever that Roosevelt endured on this trip shortened his life by many years. A wounded leg suffered abscesses; he became delirious with fever; and he lost fifty-seven pounds during the trip.

Roosevelt recovered sufficiently to travel to Madrid for Kermit's wedding. Despite his work in dismantling much of Spain's empire, Roosevelt was cordially received there.[68] He also stopped off in London, anxious to address the Royal Geographic Society, some of whose members doubted his discovery of a river almost a thousand miles long. He gave substantially the same address on June 16 in London that he had made before the National Geographic Society at Washington late in May. A map of the river with detailed explanatory remarks also appeared in the *Bulletin of the American Geographical Society*.

XV   *Editorialist of World War I*

Roosevelt, because of his increased political activities with the Progressive party, had resigned from *Outlook* in June 1914 and thereafter sent them only a few essays and reviews. In December 1914, however, he did sign a three-year contract with *Metropolitan* magazine for $25,000 a year in exchange for his articles dealing with social and political matters. When the war in Europe began, Roosevelt immediately took the side of the Allies. He began an avalanche of writing on American unpreparedness which was distributed by the Wheeler Syndicate in newspapers and by *Outlook, Everybody's*, and the *Independent*. The articles were collected in 1915 into *America and the World War*. Roosevelt feared deeply that if Germany defeated Britain, Germany would quickly become a force in South and Central America. He despaired of Wilson's ever realizing the threat to U.S. security until too late. His stand against Germany earned him many enemies, but none more acrimonious than George Sylvester Viereck, the German-American editor. *Harper's Weekly* printed an article by George Creel which attacked Roosevelt as a warmonger. But Roosevelt continued his advocacy of preparedness and increasingly lost any recognition of claims for Germany. He wrote "Lafayettes of the Air" for *Collier's* in appreciation of the first Americans in the air war in France, and his stream of articles continued in *Metropolitan*.

Roosevelt did not concern himself only with the war. He recorded strongly favorable opinions on Lady Gregory's Irish Theater; he deplored the spirit of "hyphenated" Americans who would look to their European forebears for directions in politics or art. He prepared "How Old Is Man?" for publication, but *Scribner's* and *Harper's Monthly* thought its 16,000 words too many; *National Geographic* finally published it in February 1916. He also supported the Suffrage Amendment and was sympathetic with the efforts of John L. Sullivan, the boxer, in fighting for temperance. *Fear God and Take Your Own Part* and *Holidays in the Open,* collected from his various magazine articles, also appeared at this time.

As war between the United States and Germany drew closer, Roosevelt did all in his power to get command of a division. As early as March 12, 1915, he answered a letter from William Aston Chanler by saying, "There are many worse ways of ending than in battle," and quoted "Gettysburg," by James Jeffry Roche: "To do, to dare, to die, at need." [69] Roosevelt was deeply touched by the death of his old English hunting friend Frederick Courteney Selous in combat in Africa. The great hunter at an advanced age, well over sixty, had fought for and secured a commission in the British army to fight the Germans in German East Africa, where he was killed. Roosevelt wrote one of his deepest-felt essays for *Outlook* in describing the death of Selous.

For Roosevelt the memory of his Rough Rider days, amplified by the urgency of American unpreparedness, demanded his once again going into combat. But the president and the army wanted no part of him.[70] Roosevelt persisted. He wrote to William Allen White, "As for myself, at this time I think I could do this country most good by dying in a reasonably honorable fashion, at the head of my division in the European War." [71]

Although Roosevelt did not enter the army himself, his four sons did. Quentin served in the Signal Corps as an aviator. Roosevelt urged General John Pershing to take Theodore and Archibald with the first troops to France, even if they were to go as enlisted men, though both held reserve officers' commissions. Kermit returned from his work in South America, served with the English in Mesopotamia, and then joined the American artillery in France. Roosevelt passed the period of the war in feeling useless. Occasionally he would make a speech in support of the war effort. He published *Foes of Our Household* and arranged a contract with the *Kansas City Star* at an annual salary of $25,000, also remaining associated with *Metropolitan* at $5,000. His health began to decline steadily; the fevers of Brazil returned to weaken him. In February 1918 he underwent an operation for abscesses on his thigh and his ear, which soon went deaf. Soon after he left the hospital, weakened, he learned that Archibald had been seriously wounded. Not long after, Theodore was gassed and wounded. And then Quentin was shot

down and killed. In a letter to Edith Wharton, Roosevelt wrote,
"There is no use of my writing about Quentin; for I should break
down if I tried. His death is heartbreaking. But it would have
been far worse if he had lived at the cost of the slightest failure
to perform his duty." [72] In her autobiography, Mary Roberts
Rinehart, who knew Roosevelt intimately as a friend during
World War I days, told how both were staying at the Langdon
Hotel in New York City; and when Roosevelt came into her
room, she saw him as "old." She was greatly touched by his
recitation of the loss of Quentin, and of the very important part
that his wife, Edith, played in his life.[73]

Much of the dynamic spirit of Roosevelt began to decline. He
certainly did not remain impassive, but his loss of energy was
reflected in his letters. In November he entered the hospital
again for a long stay. While he was in the hospital, the essays
he had written for the *Kansas City Star* and *Metropolitan* were
collected by Scribner's into *The Great Adventure*. He sent a
copy to Rudyard Kipling with a letter of transmittal of continued
contempt for Wilson and suspicion of the English for not seeing
through him. He then proceeded in his writing to oppose Wilson's
plans for peace, notably the League of Nations. That organi-
zation was the subject of his last essay, "The League of Nations,"
published posthumously in the *Kansas City Star* on January 13,
1919.

In the early morning of January 6, 1919, the exciting game of
The Strenuous Life ended for Theodore Roosevelt: his great
heart stopped beating.

CHAPTER 2

Historian

W HEN Theodore Roosevelt began writing his various histories, there were but twenty full-time history teachers in the
400 colleges of the United States.[1] Books of history were written
largely not by professional historians but by those labeled patricians, gentlemen, or amateur historians. The impact of the Civil
War on the consciousness of Roosevelt and his young aristocratic contemporaries led them to this preoccupation with history. The work of these men was usually marked by an earnest
effort for fairness and impartiality. The founding of the American Historical Society coincided with the gradual elimination of
all patricians from professional ranks; however, no significant
book in America was published by a professional historian prior
to the twentieth century.[2] John Higham, the historiographer,
judges: "It is clear in retrospect that amateur and professional
historians operate very differently, and that the shift from one
kind of leadership to the other has not been all clear gain." [3]
Something went out of history when the academicians took over
the writing of history from the gentlemen historians. These
amateurs seldom took themselves too seriously; they left the
imprint of personality and, sometimes, genius; none was likely
to be overwhelmed and dominated by theorists such as Marx or
Freud; and most of them wrote excellent prose.

I   The Naval War of 1812 *(1882)*

Roosevelt's *Naval War of 1812* belongs solidly among the prod-
ucts of the patrician historians. The form of the history, his
observations and comments, even his adding an additional un-
necessary chapter, typify the genius and the excesses of his
historical efforts. While still an undergraduate at Harvard,
Roosevelt was dissatisfied with all the principal accounts of the

naval war of 1812: the *Naval History of Great Britain* (1837), by the Englishman William James; James Fenimore Cooper's *Naval History of the United States* (1856); and the *Statistical History of the United States Navy* (1853), by George E. Emmons. He decided to write his own record of the war, to avoid special pleading, and by the use of every available document to present the truth in a "just" history. In his preface he lists both the sources available to him and some that were not. He began his work while still an undergraduate and published it in 1882, when he was but twenty-four.

His plan follows a purely chronological development. He opens with an introductory chapter that outlines the causes of the war and an interesting comparative survey of other accounts of the war. He then takes each year from 1812 to 1815 and describes the various battles, first on the oceans and then on the lakes between the United States and Canada. A series of appendixes, including two bibliographies, were added in later editions. In "Appendix E" Roosevelt stands by his strict judgment of the Englishman James and states in response to English criticism that "James stands convicted beyond possibility of doubt, not merely of occasional inaccuracies or errors, but of the systematic, malicious, and continuous practice of every known form of wilful misstatement, from the suppression of the truth and the suggestion of the false to the lie direct." [4] At such a young age Roosevelt declared war on the whole generation of English naval historians—and won, as later events would confirm.

The Naval War of 1812 describes in the most exquisite detail every encounter that took place during that war between any vessels on any body of water in the world. The action ranges from the British Isles to the far Pacific, from Valparaiso to the Great Lakes. The narrative involves tonnages and classifications of ships, composition of crews, armament, positions of guns, and maneuvers in combat. In explaining an encounter between any two ships, these details really comprise all that can be said of each battle; or, in some cases, such details can explain precisely why there was flight instead of combat. Whether a ship measured 1,670 tons or 1,567 tons becomes quite significant in the process of analysis. Roosevelt knew, in addition, the names of officers and crew members on both sides, and describes individual actions in the same detail that he renders to gunnery or ships' movements. His book is an imposing array of minutiae necessary for such a study. His descriptions of battles are often related in minute-by-minute accounts:

At 5.30, to keep under command and be able to wear if necessary, the *Shannon* filled her maintopsail and kept a close luff, and then again let the sail shiver. At 5.25 the *Chesapeake* hauled up her foresail, and with three ensigns flying, steered straight for the *Shannon's* starboard quarter. Broke was afraid that Lawrence would pass under the *Shannon's* stern, rake her, and engage her on the quarter; but either overlooking or waiving this advantage, the American captain luffed up within 50 yards upon the *Shannon's* starboard quarter, and squared his mainyard. On board the *Shannon* the captain of the 14th gun, William Mindham, had been ordered not to fire till it bore into the second main-deck port forward; at 5.50 it was fired, and then the other guns in quick succession from aft forward, the *Chesapeake* replying with her whole broadside. At 5.53 Lawrence, finding he was forging ahead, hauled up a little.[5]

In writing *The Naval War of 1812* Roosevelt set before himself the task of producing a just history: "Without abating a jot from one's devotion to his country and flag, I think a history can be made just enough to warrant its being received as an authority equally among Americans and Englishmen. I have endeavored to supply such a work."[6] Roosevelt chose the British naval historian William James as his chief adversary, although there were others. Roosevelt knew that James's accounts of the War of 1812 were slavishly adopted by English and Canadian authorities, who utilized them as authentic. Roosevelt sought to set the record straight. In the process he rebuked James at every opportunity. He abhorred James's "succession of acrid soliloquies on the moral defects of the American character"[7] and pointed out that since British records were not kept accurately for action on the lakes, James could let his imagination run loose. Eventually Roosevelt became hopelessly exasperated with James and remarked in a footnote: "It is monotonous work to have to supplement a history by a running commentary on James's mistakes and inventions; but it is worth while to prove once for all the utter unreliability of the author who is accepted in Great Britain as the great authority about the war."[8] Despite his exasperation, Roosevelt did not fail to go on hitting James at every opportunity. When James tried to explain away the successes of the *Wasp* before her ill-fated disappearance, Roosevelt concluded:

"Now, such a piece of writing as this is simply evidence of an unsound mind; it is not so much malicious as idiotic." [9]

Roosevelt did not write a partisan history, regardless of what had been done before him. He constantly tried to even the score when possible, pointing out the deficiencies in the American historians as well. As for the combatants, he believed that there was little difference between the Englishmen and the Americans, both coming from the same blood at that time. The successes of the Americans on the sea he attributes to freer institutions and constant practice in marksmanship. Yet he admits that the Americans could fail even when at an advantage: "It is thus seen that the *Shannon* received from shot alone only about half the damage the *Chesapeake* did; the latter was thoroughly beaten at the guns, in spite of what some American authors say to the contrary. And her victory was not in the slightest degree to be attributed to, though it may have been slightly hastened by, accident. Training and discipline won the victory, as often before; only in this instance the training and discipline were against us." [10] The captured American *Chesapeake* was towed to Halifax. Sometimes in Roosevelt's judgment the Americans failed badly, as in the battle of the *Argus* and the *Pelican*: "So that, in summing up the merits of this action, it is fair to say that both sides showed skillful seamanship and unskillful gunnery; that the British fought bravely and that the Americans did not." [11]

In writing this history, the twenty-four-year-old Roosevelt was willing to shatter past illusions. In speaking of the battle of Lake Erie, which gave American forces control of all the upper lakes, Roosevelt cautions against placing Captain Perry on too high a level of fame for his achievement: "He certainly stands on a lower grade than either Hull or Macdonough, and not a bit higher than a dozen others." [12] His revisionism also comes down terribly hard on Jefferson and Madison for their unpreparedness, but especially on Jefferson for his strange ideas of naval defense by gunboats.

Furthermore, Roosevelt reaches an interesting conclusion in his history. He states that nothing done by the American navy could have materially affected the result of the war. The struggle on the oceans was merely a matter of individual cruises and fights. The victories kept up the spirit of the American people and gave the nation a worldwide reputation. National honor

came by a few single-ship duels; the United States won Free
Trade and Sailors' Rights.

The Naval War of 1812 caught the attention of historians on
both sides of the Atlantic approvingly. The *New York Times*
reviewer wrote: "The volume is an excellent one in every respect,
and shows in so young an author the best promise for a good
historian—fearlessness of statement, caution, endeavor to be im-
partial, and a brisk and interesting way of telling events. It may
be thoroughly recommended to take the place of more classical
but less accurate accounts of the naval war of 1812." [13]

The book was so fair and so accurate that the English historian William Laird Clowes asked Roosevelt to write that portion of *The Royal Navy from Earliest Times to the Present*
which dealt with the war of 1812. Roosevelt accepted, thereby
winning his war with the school of William James. The offer
prompted an objection by a reviewer for *Macmillan's Magazine*
in 1898 to an American's writing any portion of a history of the
British navy. The reviewer began in caustic fashion: "Following
a fashion rather prevalent of late years, though almost incom-
patible with the production of literature, it is the work of a
society of gentlemen, whose chief and director is Mr. Laird
Clowes." [14] The author sees Clowes as having his eyes on the
American market, yet he constantly repeats that Roosevelt is
fair in his treatment of the British. He challenges Roosevelt's
claim that peer institutions made superior sailors; after all, the
same institutions produced the craven militia of whom Roosevelt
spoke with humiliation. The reviewer convincingly demonstrates
that Britain's obligations around the world at the time made
necessary the use of inexperienced seamen. He accuses Roosevelt
of ignoring the facts that American hulls were distinctly thicker,
and that American guns were mounted higher above the water
line. He acknowledges, however, that the English neglected gunnery practice to emphasize "spit and polish." He concludes gra-
ciously: "But we have not the least wish to quarrel with Mr.
Roosevelt. On the contrary we cheerfully allow that his book
contains much useful information and many shrewd remarks, that
it is by comparison fair, and is nearly always free from the
uneasy self-assertion and underbred measuring of themselves
with others which is an unpleasant feature of much American
writing. Our objection is not to Mr. Roosevelt as a writer for

Americans and in America; it is to his appearance in the list of contributors to a history of the Royal Navy. . . ." [15]

Roosevelt made an unfortunate addition to the third edition of *The Naval War of 1812*. Unable to accept the ignominy of the land war, Roosevelt chose not to write a book about that subject as he had planned, but simply to add an account of the great victory at New Orleans. In this added chapter he sees the southern land war as a last attempt, as well, for the Indian tribes to stop the advance of the Americans to the West. A victory for the English would have given a reprieve to the Indian nationalities. Jackson broke the back of the Creek confederacies, then drove the Spanish from Pensacola, and finally started west to defend New Orleans. From this point on, Roosevelt overwrites his narrative. The tone is completely different from the first twelve chapters. He was so very proud that the Americans had routed the British troops who had defeated Napoleon that he romantically wrote their story to help forget the disgraceful American defeats in the East. His writing becomes excessive and affected: "Many a sword, till then but a glittering toy, was that night crusted with blood." [16] And he writes: "There stood the matchless infantry of the island king, in the pride of their strength and the splendor of their martial glory; and as the haze cleared away they moved forward, in stern silence, broken only by the angry, snarling notes of the brazen bugles." [17] The picturesque earnestness of this chapter led the reviewer for the *New York Times* to say of this section, "Mr. Roosevelt writes less like a professional historian than a very bright-minded and enthusiastic gentleman who pursues the study of history as something more than a hobby and something less than a profession." [18] Happily, Roosevelt dropped the romance and recovered his objectivity, as far as he was ever able, in writing *The Winning of the West*.

II   The Winning of the West *(1889–1896)*

In planning *The Winning of the West*, Roosevelt fully intended to carry his investigations from the East all the way to Florida and thence to Oregon, Texas, New Mexico, and California. Actually, he completed four volumes, and these cover what is now Kentucky, Tennessee, Illinois, Ohio, and Indiana. He traveled to all parts of the United States, often on horseback, to gather materials for his books. Although William Frederick Poole in a review of the first two volumes for the *Atlantic Monthly* in 1889 wrote, "No man, whatever may be his ability or industry, —even if he is a ranchman,—can write a history in its best form on horseback," [19] what resulted has been authoritatively called one of the five major works on American history produced in the last quarter of the nineteenth century.[20]

The Winning of the West is told in a series of lively and dramatic narratives, each necessarily loosely connected or even loosely related to the others, inasmuch as this looseness was the nature of the prodigious expansion. In his history, the first portion of the narrative describes the spasmodic movement into the eastern watershed of the Mississippi during the period from 1763 to 1807; without this expansion the boundaries of the United States of America would be just about what they had been in 1763. Roosevelt gets the region on chronological line in his first five chapters by describing the spread of the English-speaking peoples, the French in the northern Ohio Valley, the Indian confederacies in the Appalachians, the Algonquins in the northwest territory, and the perilous adventures of the hunters and surveyors in the most western Alleghenies. The backwoodsmen, exemplified by Daniel Boone, were the first to violate the admonitions and restrictions of the British king. Roosevelt next describes the work of George Rogers Clark at Vincennes, the Moravian Massacre, and the activities of the Revolutionary War in the Holston settlements. He closes the first two volumes with James Robertson's accomplishments in the Cumberland settlements up to 1783.

Having brought his history through the Revolutionary War, Roosevelt in his next two volumes concerns himself with even more complex matters. He explains the inrush of settlers, mainly adventurous veterans of the Revolutionary War; the continuing Indian wars in the Northwest; St. Clair's defeat; the movement into statehood by Kentucky and Tennessee; and the subtle resistance to the southwestern expansion by Spain. Boundary definitions involved claims directly west to the Mississippi River by states along their northernmost and southernmost latitudes, even Connecticut claiming land west of Pennsylvania. Roosevelt's firm grasp in understanding the events of land speculation heighten the drama of the John Jay treaty with England and the Thomas Pickney treaty with Spain. He ends his history with the story of the purchase of Louisiana and Aaron Burr's conspiracy, followed by the great explorations of the Far West by Meriwether Lewis, William Clark, and Zebulon Montgomery Pike.

Roosevelt demonstrates that the period from 1763 to 1807 changed the aspect and destiny of the United States from a small, self-contained, populated strip along a narrow portion of the continent on the Atlantic to a nation that had no idea of how great it would grow except that it would grow. He captures the excitement of this new national spirit which converted huge traces of geography into a single nation with a united purpose: to seize and hold the land from European and Indian. His history is the story of military conquest and the spread of civilization. Roosevelt learned some of his methodology from Francis Parkman, but his own intimate knowledge of frontier life and his regard for what the American settler represented made his own studies quite distinct. In *The Winning of the West* more than anywhere else, Roosevelt bridges the gap between the patrician and the scientific historian, retaining the best of each. On the one hand his volumes are an exemplary rendition of carefully documented historical facts; on the other, they are full of astute opinions on matters of allied interest, especially his reading of men's characters. He does not hesitate to commend or challenge one historian after another, being particularly hard on those who believed too much of what they heard from supposed eye-witness observers.

When the *New York Times* reported that Roosevelt "eschews sentimentality," [21] the significant truth about this history is clearly stated: he berates older historians; he holds strong opinions on race; he has little sympathy for savages; he abhors the pacifism of the Moravian converts; and he accepts the law of the frontier. He tries over and over to convince the reader that people and not individual leaders won the West. He points out that "armed hunters, wood-choppers, and farmers were their own soldiers. They built and manned their own forts; they did their own fighting under their own commanders. There were no regiments of regular troops along the frontier." [22] And though he gives an admirable portrait of Daniel Boone, he adds:

Boone is interesting as a leader and explorer; but he is still more interesting as a type. The West was neither discovered, won, nor settled by any single man. No keen-eyed statesman planned the movement, nor was it carried out by any great military leader; it was the work of a whole people, of whom each man was impelled mainly by sheer love of adventure; it was the outcome of the ceaseless strivings of all the dauntless, restless backwoods folk to win homes for their descendants and to each penetrate deeper than his neighbors into the remote forest hunting grounds where the perilous pleasures of the chase and of war could be best enjoyed. We owe the conquest of the West to all the backwoodsmen, not to any solitary individual among them; where all alike were strong and daring there was no chance for any single man to rise to unquestioned pre-eminence.[23]

Still, when the reader finishes, he will have the deepest regard for George Rogers Clark, Daniel Boone, James Robertson, John Sevier, and Kasper Mansker.

No book written by an American could be less sympathetic to the Indians. Although some Indians were semicivilized and some chiefs owned Negro slaves, most were less than barbarians, and merely savages. Their cruelties to the whites included many brutal acts too horrible to mention, Roosevelt says, despite the striking examples he does provide: "The settler and pioneer have at bottom had justice on their side; this great continent could not have been kept as nothing but a game-preserve for squalid savages." [24] However, he respects the fighting abilities of the Indians and firmly believes that no band of Indians was ever defeated by an inferior force. As far as real-estate holdings were concerned, no one Indian tribe could claim ownership to any particular tract; each held what he had until it was taken from him. This was the law among the Indians; the white man adopted this rule as his own. But the white man fortified his settlements and held on.

Most of Roosevelt's history concentrates on the wars with the Indians, but nothing of importance escapes him. He describes Lord Dunmore's War, Clark's fantastic conquest of Illinois, the Watauga or Holston settlements, the commonwealth of Transylvania, the state of Franklin, the veterans of the Revolution, the allure of land speculation, and the success of Anthony Wayne— every story in exciting, proud, and appreciative understanding.

The listing of events hardly conveys what makes *The Winning of the West* such a notable contribution to American historical literature. Roosevelt's hatred of slavery, his theories concerning the Revolution and the founding of the nation, his disdain for Jefferson, his intense aversion to separatist movements, and a thousand digressions and impressions keep these volumes from ever becoming dull. True, he harps occasionally on a particular point and becomes repetitious, yet on the whole his lively history keeps moving. Roosevelt wants to be sure of his facts; and his fairness to all, except perhaps to the Spanish, is stamped on every page.

William Dean Howells, as editor of the *Atlantic Monthly*, asked William Frederick Poole, president of the young American Historical Association, to review the first volumes published by Putnam's for his magazine. Poole had written scholarly historical articles on the West and also had been president of the American Library Association. He appreciated Roosevelt's natural, simple, picturesque style, and his methodology. But he wished that Roosevelt had made use of the Haldimand Collection at Ottawa to understand fully the raid of Captain Byrd from Detroit into Kentucky and its relation to operations on the Mississippi. He insisted on giving Virginians much more credit for the conquest of the Northwest than did Roosevelt, and he objected to Roosevelt's comments on previous historians. [25]

True to his custom and anxious to be informed, Roosevelt wrote to the anonymous reviewer of the *Atlantic Monthly* and acknowledged the justice of some of the criticism. He also pointed out that, upon accepting the appointment as Civil Service Commissioner, he had to get the history out at once or wait several years and added, "I ought to have done the latter, I suppose,—but I didn't." [26] He regretted that he had never met a man with whom he could discuss the western history in its entirety.

Poole thanked Roosevelt for his polite letter. He confessed that he knew no one in the East familiar with western history. After saying, "You have entered a fresh and most interesting field of research, and I predict for you a great success," [27] he went on to offer Roosevelt his notes and asked him to read various articles which Poole had previously published. Roosevelt answered, "What I am especially aiming at in my history is to present the important facts, and yet to avoid being drowned in a mass of detail. It is hard to strike the 'just middle' between hastiness on the one hand and intolerable antiquarian minuteness on the other." [28]

Roosevelt met Poole at the 1889 meeting of the American Historical Association. At this meeting Roosevelt gave an extempore address in which he deplored the ignorance in the East of the grand and meaningful history of the West. He found such ignorance not unlike that of the English regarding American history in general. He then proceeded to trace the excitement of the western migration, to prove that American history is as dramatic as any history in the world. A lively controversy followed over the matter of permanent settlements beyond the Alleghenies before the Revolution. Dr. Toner of the Congressional Library, Dr. Stillé of Philadelphia, and Poole supported the concept; Roosevelt and Edward G. Mason, president of the Chicago Historical Society, insisted as a general proposition that there were no such settlements. [29] Roosevelt could argue on his feet with the best professional historians in the country. Once again, his love of controversy began to move others into activity.

III The Rough Riders (1899)

Theodore Roosevelt not only wrote studies of history, he also participated in the making of history. During the Spanish-American War he did both. His story of the campaign in Cuba prompted the image of Roosevelt that has generally been perpetuated throughout the years. The name of Theodore Roosevelt inevitably arouses the image of the colonel and his charge up San Juan Hill with the Rough Riders. In reality, Roosevelt did not charge up San Juan Hill; he charged up Kettle Hill, which was near but behind San Juan Hill, in the battle for Santiago. The hundred days' war with Spain had its serious side, yet it had aspects that now seem ludicrous. The humorous nature of the war did not escape Finley Peter Dunne, a perceptive contemporary columnist, who suggested alternate titles for *The Rough Riders*, such as "Alone in Cubia," "The Biography iv a Hero be Wan who Knows," "The Darin' Exploits iv a Brave Man be an Actual Eye Witness," "Th' Account iv th' Desthruction iv Spanish Power in th' Ant Hills, as it fell fr'm th' lips of Teddy Rosenfelt an' was took down be his own hands." [30] The Rough Riders did not really ride in battle at all; except for the officers' horses, the remainder of the animals had been left behind in Florida.

The press coverage of the First U.S. Volunteer Cavalry, Roosevelt's unit, gave as much attention to the Ivy League College recruits of the outfit as they did to the wild riders and riflemen of the Rockies and Great Plains, where the regiment was supposed to have been raised. Transportation arrangements failed to materialize after the regiment arrived in Tampa from Texas, and the unit had to fend for itself:

It was four days later that we disembarked, in a perfect welter of confusion. Tampa lay in the pine-covered sandflats at the end of a one-track railroad, and everything connected with both military and railroad matters was in an almost inextricable tangle. There was no one to meet us or to tell us where we were to camp, and no one to issue us food for the first twenty-four hours; while the railroad people unloaded us wherever they pleased, or rather wherever the jam of all kinds of trains rendered it possible. We had to buy the men food out of our own pockets, and to seize wagons in order to get our spare baggage taken to the camping-ground which we at last found had been allotted to us.[31]

When it was time to leave Tampa for Cuba, eight troops of seventy men each were taken; four troops stayed behind, many of these bursting into tears of disappointment. When the regiment arrived at the track designated for a train to Port Tampa, no train moved. Roosevelt and the other officers queried brigadier generals and even a major general, but none knew what was going on. Whether a regiment boarded a train or not made little difference, because still no train moved. Roosevelt's regiment received orders to move to another track, but no train appeared there. In the late afternoon some coal cars came by, and with various arguments the engineer was persuaded to take the regiment nine miles to Port Tampa, where they arrived ready for war, covered with coal dust. No one could tell the next step with the economy of Roosevelt's narrative:

At last, however, after over an hour's industrious and rapid search through this swarming ant-heap of humanity, Wood [Colonel Leonard Wood, the commander of the Rough Riders; Roosevelt was second-in-command.] and I, who had separated, found Colonel Humphrey at nearly the same time and were allotted a transport—the *Yucatan*. She was out in midstream, so Wood seized a stray launch and boarded her. At the same time I happened to find out that she had previously been allotted to two other regiments—the Second Regular Infantry and the Seventy-first New York Volunteers, which latter regiment alone contained more men than could be put aboard her. Accordingly, I ran at full speed to our train; and leaving a strong guard with the baggage, I double-quicked the rest of the regiment up to the boat, just in time to board her as she came into the quay, and then to hold her against the Second Regulars and the Seventy-first, who had arrived a little too late, being a shade less ready than we were in the matter of individual initiative.[32]

From the arrival in Tampa to boarding the overcrowded transport had taken thirty-six "tolerably active" hours. Now the rations on board were not only insufficient, they were inedible for the most part, and in the steaming heat of June the transport rested in the harbor at Tampa for six days in the blazing sun. Finally the invasion force of thirty transports moved out for a six-day trip to Cuba. The men worked their way to the Cuban shore in a heavy surf; the horses and mules were simply thrown overboard to swim to shore as best they could. One of Roosevelt's horses drowned.

When the first firing began, the regulars acted with cool deliberation; not one man stopped to assist the wounded. The regulars had not a single straggler; their fire discipline was so perfect that they expended not over ten rounds per man. When some of the regular officers were wounded, they continued to advance their men and would permit no one to assist them. However, the Rough Riders had a most inauspicious first combat action. The pace set by Colonel Leonard Wood, their commander, was too hard for them. Some dropped their bundles; others fell out of line and became stragglers. Yet Wood had to press on to assist the regulars, who were routing the Spanish defenders.

From that time forward the officers of the Rough Riders were determined to have their men follow the example set by the regulars. "No man was allowed to drop out to help the wounded. It was hard to leave them there in the jungle, where they might not be found again until the vultures or land-crabs came, but war is a grim game and there was no choice." [33] Roosevelt himself learned fast as well; when he didn't know what to do, he charged: "I was still very much in the dark as to where the main body of the Spanish forces were, or exactly what lines the battle was following, and was very uncertain what I ought to do; but I knew it could not be wrong to go forward, and I thought I would find Wood and then see what he wished me to do. I was in a mood to cordially welcome guidance, for it was most bewildering to fight an enemy whom one so rarely saw." [34] Wood provided an excellent example for Roosevelt, who felt compelled to emulate him:

"How Wood escaped being hit, I do not see, and still less how
his horse escaped. I had left mine at the beginning of the action,
and was only regretting that I had not left my sword with it, as
it kept getting between my legs when I was tearing my way
through the jungle. I never wore it again in action." [35]

Roosevelt's book does as well as has ever been done in recording the dumb confusion of men under heavy fire. Casualties
began to accumulate; heroism appeared on every side. One
man, part Cherokee, suffered six wounds in half an hour but
refused to leave the line until a seventh bullet caused him to
lose too much blood. Another man crawled out of his hospital
cot into the jungle to evade the ambulance ride to the rear. A
West Point Cadet, Ernest Haskell, who had taken his holiday
with the regiment as acting second lieutenant, distinguished
himself but was shot through the stomach.

As Roosevelt's narrative continues it becomes more incredible.
It is not comic; it is not absurd; it is not even simply real. If
anything, in some mysterious way it is more real than reality;
it is reality lived and explained on some higher level of experience than exists in the ordinary world of men and their affairs.
Death and injury become so commonplace as to be deprived of
their pain. Action becomes a stunned, automatic response.
Roosevelt's eye for detail and his power of total recall bring alive
every moment of each encounter with the enemy. Up Kettle
Hill he went, leading now not only his own troops, but also
various regular units, including the black troopers of the Ninth
Regiment. When most needed, Lieutenant John H. Parker arrived
with his Gatling guns. [36] Roosevelt suffered a slight wound; he
killed a Spanish soldier; he continued to take command of any
soldiers without officers; and he continued to charge. When the
Army later refused to give Roosevelt a division in World War I,
their decision is totally understandable from the Army's point
of view. Roosevelt was a one-man army; he operated outside
the routines of paperwork and procedures.

After the victory, the usual letdown of ennui and anticlimax
followed. The job done, everyone wanted to return home. Washington had other plans. The men lingered on in Cuba, now more
threatened by fever than by bullets. At one point only 50 percent
of the regiment was fit for duty. A good soldier would sometimes die, whereas a malingerer would recover. Roosevelt es-

caped the fever and, with the urging of other officers, managed to persuade the army to bring the men home. The United States would never see such a regiment again.

Roosevelt's record of the Rough Riders can stand beside any book of combat ever written by an American. It may not have the lyrical qualities of Stephen Crane's imaginary *Red Badge of Courage*, but it is far richer in the actual, physical descriptions of battle. Roosevelt's style is rough, direct, and unadorned. Whereas Crane's novel is a study of triumph over fear, Roosevelt's recitation of true events has nothing of fear in them. The sacrifice and bravery of the men can only be explained by Roosevelt's constant claim that it was a "people's war." The men involved willingly put their lives on the line for what they believed was their duty to humanity. There is nothing of bombast or histrionics in *The Rough Riders*; Roosevelt showed great restraint in telling his story of the war, tempered no doubt by the nearness of the events.

IV *Three Biographies*

Every biographer imposes his personal mark on the work he produces. In some instances the effect is slight, in others, quite apparent. Some biographies can hardly be called history at all. In writing his biographies of Thomas Hart Benton, Gouverneur Morris, and Oliver Cromwell, Theodore Roosevelt stood closer to the tradition of Plutarch than to James Boswell. Roosevelt promoted his own ideas of political philosophy and attacked the ideas of his adversaries through the medium of biography; he did not strive for comprehensive, detailed treatment of his biographical subjects. His biographies contain his own interpretations of history, his own political thought, and the plain stamp of his personality.

Thomas Hart Benton (1887)

In the biography of Senator Hart Benton of Missouri, Roosevelt faithfully portrays the essential character and achievements of the man who was born in North Carolina, matured in Tennessee, and then as senator from Missouri figured so importantly in the war on the Bank of the United States and in other currency matters during the administrations of Andrew Jackson and Martin Van Buren. Benton's support was important in the movement west. Roosevelt in his study concentrates on two important beliefs held by Benton, both most dear to Roosevelt himself—his belief in Manifest Destiny, and his love and devotion to the Union. Roosevelt respects Benton deeply for his high moral courage and the great personal sacrifice that Benton made of his political career to preserve the Union. Although a slave-holder, Benton, in Roosevelt's analysis, is more a westerner than a southerner in his thinking. Where Benton allied himself with the South and slavery, he did so with the belief in gradual, peaceful emancipation.

Roosevelt resembled Benton in many ways, and he agreed with him strongly on many, but not all, political positions. Benton was a man of tremendous energies, and he "possessed such phenomenal power of application and study, and his capacity for and his delight in work were so extraordinary, that he was able to grapple with many . . . subjects of importance, and to present them in a way that showed he had thoroughly mastered them both in principal and detail. . . ." [37] Benton read widely, and was complimented by Daniel Webster for knowing more political facts than any man in Washington and for possessing a wonderful fund of general knowledge. Roosevelt admires Benton too for his hard stand on the Indian problem, so much so that Benton's policies lead Roosevelt to write: "The Sioux and Cheyennes, for instance, have more often been sinning than sinned against; for example, the so-called Chivington or Sandy Creek Massacre, in spite of certain most objectionable details, was on the whole as righteous and beneficial a deed as ever took place on the frontier." [38] Roosevelt also points out that Benton always insisted on jury trials for blacks and held out for immigrants to own land before becoming naturalized. Benton vigorously opposed nullification; he supported Jackson in the bank dispute; he fought for fair borderlines with Canada; he was hated by businessmen; he thought the war with Mexico unjust. All these political positions endeared Benton to Roosevelt, who makes his subject into a greater man in his later years than anyone of his time, despite Benton's being defeated for U.S. Representative and the governorship of Missouri in his final years.

But Roosevelt does not adulate Benton. He thinks Benton's

commitment to dueling "either absurd, trivial, or wholly incom-
prehensible," [39] and is sometimes annoyed by his pedantry and
pretentiousness: "Unfortunately Benton would interlard even his
best speeches with theories of economics often more or less
crude, and, still worse, with a series of classic quotations and
allusions; for he was grievously afflicted with the rage for cheap
pseudo-classicism that Jefferson and his school had borrowed
from the French revolutionists." [40] In a more serious vein,
Benton's strict interpretation of the Constitution, or loose interpretation of the Constitution, howsoever it pleased him, Roosevelt labels ridiculous, "when on his ultrademocratic hobby
Benton always rode very loose in the saddle, and with little
knowledge of where he was going." [41] Roosevelt also calls Benton
to task for his extreme philosophical position on democracy:

He was an enthusiastic believer in the extreme Jeffersonian doctrinaire
views as to the will of the majority being always right, and as to the
moral perfection of the average voter. Like his fellow statesmen he
failed to see the curious absurdity of supporting black slavery, and
yet claiming universal suffrage for whites as a divine right, not as a
mere matter of expediency resulting on the whole better than any
other method. He had not learned that the majority in a democracy
has no more right to tyrannize over a minority than, under a different
system, the latter would have to oppress the former; and that, if there
is a moral principle at stake, the saying that the voice of the people
is the voice of God may be quite as untrue, and do quite as much
mischief, as the old theory of the divine right of kings.[42]

Benton's life and political career furnish Roosevelt the opportunity to comment on U.S. history of the period 1820 to 1860.
The tariff, hard money, nullification, the banks, slavery, the
spoils system, abolitionists, Jacksonian democracy, all come
under examination and comment. Roosevelt is rarely kind in
speaking of the presidents of this period. Of Van Buren he says,
"He succeeded because of, and not in spite of, his moral shortcomings; if he had always governed his actions by a high moral
standard he would probably never have been heard of." [43]
Franklin Pierce is "a small politician, of low capacity and mean
surroundings, proud to act as the servile tool of men worse than
himself but also stronger and abler." [44] John Tyler, the "politician of monumental littleness," Roosevelt classifies as a confused

man: "His peevishness, vacillation, ambitious vanity, and sheer puzzle-headedness made him incline first to the side of his new friends and present supporters, the Whigs, and then to that of his old Democratic allies. . . ." [45] Jackson is the "ignorant, headstrong, and straight-forward soldier." [46] Roosevelt asserts, "Jefferson was the father of nullification, and therefore of secession," [47] and is gratified that "one result, at least, the Nullifiers accomplished—they completely put an end to the Jefferson birthday celebrations." [48] Because of Zachary Taylor's stand on Union, Roosevelt has kind words for him: "He was neither a great statesman nor yet a great commander; but he was an able and gallant soldier, a loyal and upright public servant, and a most kindly, honest, and truthful man. His death was a greater loss to the country than perhaps the people knew." [49]

Roosevelt's final words on Benton commend him for his steady growth of character to the last, for his great learning, for his ten years of devotion to his paralytic wife, and, last, for holding "every good gift he had completely at the service of the American Federal Union." [50]

The vigor of Roosevelt's writing led a New York reviewer to state:

The author combines sympathy with cool-headedness in a remarkable degree. He writes disinterestedly, and yet is moved by a strong sense of justice. His style, however, is not restful, calm, and smooth. It rather partakes of the animation and tempestuousness of the times about which he is writing. The volume has more the character, so far as form goes, of a political pamphlet than of a polished essay. It is stirring, argumentative, bold. Readers of a future time might question if it were not written in Benton's own day, so infused is it with literary vigor and the breeze of politics. [51]

Roosevelt's study of Benton admittedly goes beyond Benton himself and becomes a political history of the times in which Benton lived. Still, essentially little more remains to be said of Benton's career except minor details or revealing anecdotes which Roosevelt did not include. A curious twist has actually occurred with the passing of years. The writer of the biography himself became a vastly more important historical figure than his subject. And the life of Benton can be read not only for the light it throws on the political thought of a young man of

twenty-nine who would become the first modern President of
the United States, but also for the way that the example and
thought of Benton helped to form that president.

Gouverneur Morris (1888)

In his study of Gouverneur Morris Roosevelt concentrates solely on the major achievements of Morris: "He made the final
draft of the United States Constitution; he first outlined our
present system of national coinage; he originated and got under
way the plan for the Erie Canal; as a minister to France he
successfully performed the most difficult task ever allotted to
an American representative at a foreign capital." [52] But Roosevelt did not have access to Morris's personal papers, and this
biography contains far more of Roosevelt's thought on this early
period of American history than it does Morris's.

Roosevelt has the deepest regard for the services Morris gave
to his country; however, there are serious issues on which Roosevelt will not justify the stand taken by his subject. Roosevelt
admires Morris first of all for his decision to work for the Revolution against the sympathies of his Tory family. Because of his
family's loyalty to the crown, Morris was "regarded with suspicion by the baser spirits in the American party." [53] When interest began to wane in New England for support of Washington's army, Morris tried valiantly to secure better pay for the
officers of the army. Morris also wins Roosevelt's approval for
his contemptuous treatment of Thomas Paine. Roosevelt was
among those who would not forgive Paine for his anti-Christian
sentiments expressed in *The Age of Reason,* and certainly not
for his contemptuous *Letter to Washington.* Paine lingered long
in a French prison before the Americans influenced his release.
Roosevelt says, "Morris refused to interfere too actively, judging
rightly that Paine would be saved by his own insignificance and
would serve his own interests best by keeping still. So the filthy
little atheist had to stay in prison 'where he amused himself
with publishing a pamphlet against Jesus Christ.'" [64] In quoting
Morris here, Roosevelt is faithfully recording the response to
Paine which made him an outcast upon his return to America.
Paine will always be a controversial historical figure, but there
is no doubt of the position taken by Morris or Roosevelt on
Paine. Roosevelt continues to commend Morris for his clear and
sound judgments on the period of the French Revolution. Morris

was actually a counselor of the court and even participated in a scheme to save the king and queen, thwarted only by the king's failure of nerve. Roosevelt says admiringly of him:

Perhaps there has hardly been another instance where, in such a crisis, the rulers have clutched in their despair at the advice of a mere private stranger sojourning in the land on his own business. The king and his ministers, as well as the queen, kept in constant communication with him. With Montmorin he dined continually, and was consulted at every stage. But he could not prevail on them to adopt the bold, vigorous measures he deemed necessary; his plain speaking startled them, and they feared it would not suit the temper of the people. He drafted numerous papers for them, among others a royal speech, which the king liked, but which his ministers prevented him from using.[55]

Morris held two political positions that caused Roosevelt some pain, yet even so Roosevelt's sense of fairness pervades his judgment of Morris. Morris feared and dreaded the growth of the West and at the Constitutional Convention did all that he could to keep the West subordinate to the East; in the late years of his career he espoused the northern disunion movement among the Federalists inspired during the War of 1812. Nothing in political activity could be more abhorrent than the latter to Roosevelt, by this time a severe nationalist. Roosevelt never hesitated to chastize the Northeast for its sectionalism and superciliousness. At several points in his biography of Benton, he rebukes New England for its loss of militancy and bemoans the noncombative sympathies of the Quakers. The Northeast, he contends, has been cautious and timid in its way of looking at possible foreign wars, and shares none of the expansionist drives to the West. Roosevelt also condemns out-of-hand the abolitionists of the Northeast who ultimately made no contribution to the winning of the Civil War or the elimination of slavery. Roosevelt is especially forceful in his stand against the actions of the abolitionists. His opinion in *Benton* of New England is stated thus: "New England was not only the most advanced portion of the Union, as regards intelligence, culture, and general prosperity, but was also most disagreeably aware of the fact, and was possessed with a self-conscious virtue that was peculiarly irritating to Westerners, who knew that they were looked down upon, and savagely resented it on every occasion; and, besides,

New England was apt to meddle in affairs that more nearly concerned other localities." [56]

Roosevelt attributes Morris's perversion of national purpose to his affiliation with the ultra-Federalists of New York, allied with those in New England. Roosevelt argues that the War of 1812 was "distinctly worth fighting and resulted in good to the country." [57] The weakness and indecision in the conduct of the war created hardships and losses that could have been avoided. Roosevelt insists that Morris's fierce opposition to the war and his hatred of the opposite party actually caused him to lose loyalty to the United States. Morris championed the British impressment of seamen from American ships; he approved British offers of peace which would have closed the West to the new nation; and even countenanced the creation of Indian nations under the protection of Britain. Morris could take no pleasure in American victories because each victory spited his political positions. Roosevelt expands the list of Morris's offenses and the actions of the Federalist leaders toward disloyalty to the Union, and reminds his readers of the disunion movement later among northern abolitionists led by William Lloyd Garrison.

Despite his objections to the later politics of Morris, Roosevelt finds much to admire in him, particularly in his behavior during the days of terror in Paris, when Morris provided refuge and escape for scores of people. Roosevelt had no respect for the corrupt French aristocracy; however, he concludes his judgment of Morris's account of the fall of the monarchy in this way: "No one of Morris's countrymen can read his words even now without feeling a throb of pride in the dead statesman who, a century ago, held up so high the honor of his nation's name in the times when souls of all but the very bravest were tried and found wanting." [58] He acknowledges Morris's prominent part in the Constitutional Convention, sees in his speeches the shortcomings of Morris's gifts, and identifies the reason that Morris never rose to the first rank of statesmen: "His keen, masterful mind, his farsightedness, and the force and subtlety of his reasoning were all marred by his incurable cynicism and deep-rooted distrust of mankind. He throughout appears as *advocatus diaboli*; he puts the lowest interpretation upon every act, and frankly avows his disbelief in all generous and unselfish motives." [59] Roosevelt's opinions on the actions of Morris and the history of the period flash out on almost every page of this biography.

No book ever written could contain more clauses such as "he was right" or "he was wrong"; for example, "He wished to deny to the small States the equal representation in the Senate finally allowed them; and he was undoubtedly right theoretically";[60] and "Morris championed a strong national government, wherein he was right; but he also championed a system of class representation, leaning toward aristocracy, wherein he was wrong." [61] Roosevelt passes judgments on Morris and American history and French history without trepidation. These traits demonstrate that for Roosevelt history was a living enterprise to which he could respond out of his own political and moral judgment; such judgments make his biographies unique. Further, these comments by Roosevelt demonstrate the uses of history in order that history need not repeat itself. There is no dry-as-dust history in this biography; there is as much of Roosevelt as there is of Morris.

Oliver Cromwell (1900)

Roosevelt's *Oliver Cromwell* consists of only 150 pages in Volume X of his *Works*. Roosevelt produced the book while he was Governor of New York, dictating most of it at various times in his busy day. In many respects it is the most analytical of his biographies, as fresh and stimulating as when it first appeared in serial form in 1900. Roosevelt begins with a survey of the times and the man, goes into the complicated business of the Long Parliament, describes closely the events of the Second Civil War and the death of Charles I, proceeds to the Irish and Scots Wars, examines the Commonwealth and the Protectorate, and closes with Cromwell's personal rule of England.

Cromwell still elicits more complex reactions at the mention of his name than does, perhaps, any other Englishman. The fear of controversy over his subject did not deter Roosevelt; he considers Cromwell "the greatest Englishman of the seventeenth century" on the first page of his study, and "by far the greatest ruler of England" on the last. Roosevelt had a firm vision of Cromwell's motives and objectives and transmits them unabashedly throughout the book. Roosevelt takes the view that he, Roosevelt, knows what is noble and what is ignoble in this world, and such a tone coincides quite often with the character of Cromwell himself. People who feared Roosevelt for his righteousness and moral preachments could easily see enough of

Roosevelt in the tyranny of Cromwell to give them pause. In any number of paragraphs the name Roosevelt could be substituted for Cromwell to trace the author's career: "It cannot too often be repeated that, whether in the end Cromwell's ambitions did or did not obscure the high principles with which they certainly blended, yet he rose to supreme power less by his own volition than by the irresistible march of events, and because he was 'a man of the mighty days, and equal to the days.'" [62] Furthermore, in many respects the amateur soldiers who comprised the Rough Riders of '98 corresponded precisely with the saints of Cromwell's army: "There is nothing sacrosanct in the trade of the soldier. It is a trade which can be learned without special difficulty by any man who is brave and intelligent, who realizes the necessity of obedience, and who is already gifted with physical hardihood and is accustomed to the use of the horse and of weapons, to enduring fatigue and exposure, and to acting on his own responsibility, taking care of himself in the open." [63] The Rough Riders and Cromwell's army were formed of these same elemental traits.

Roosevelt often explains away Cromwell's hypocrisy, commends him for horrors, and never questions the man's sanity; yet he criticizes Cromwell for supposedly knowing heaven's will better than other men might know it, for not forming a legal and constitutional system to avoid evils, for his dictatorial habit of mind, and for regression in theory of government to that professed by his predecessors. Roosevelt persists in his infatuation with Cromwell because he sees him as the leader of the greatest epoch of the English-speaking world, the first modern, and not the last medieval, movement: "Fundamentally, it was the first struggle for religious, political, and social freedom, as we now understand the terms." [64]

All through his biography of Cromwell, Roosevelt makes comparisons and contrasts with the American Civil War and the American Revolutionary War, from the inception of these wars to their conclusions; and he does the same with the men involved in these wars. It may seem strange to read, "Eliot, Hampden, and Pym stood for the principles that were championed by Washington, Patrick Henry, and the Adamses"; [65] but Roosevelt is convincingly demonstrating that the grievances which forced the Long Parliament to bloodshed are the same that made the Continental Congress ambush and destroy the forces of

George III to end his sovereignty over the Thirteen Colonies. "In neither case was there the kind of grinding tyranny which has led to the assassination of tyrants and the frantic, bloodthirsty uprising of tortured slaves. In each case the tyranny was in its first stage not its last; but the reason for this was simply that a nation of vigorous freemen will always revolt by the time the first stage has been reached." [66]

Roosevelt makes like comparisons with the great leaders of the Civil War in the United States; and in comparing the men and events, he usually faults Cromwell and his allies. In one instance he tells of the magnanimity of Abraham Lincoln in the summer of 1864, willing to accept a Democratic victory and the election of General George McClellan to the presidency. Lincoln, says Roosevelt, made every possible arrangement for the transition of power because Lincoln put the preservation of the Union above all other considerations. Whereas Cromwell had less reason to seize and hold power than did Lincoln, Cromwell chose the wrong way: "Great man though he was, and far though the good that he did outbalanced the evil, yet he lost the right to stand with men like Washington and Lincoln of modern times, and with the very, very few who, like Timoleon, in some measure approached their standard in ancient times." [67]

One of Roosevelt's important points, perhaps repeated too often, is that ordinary men can be molded into great leaders and excellent soldiers, but that ordinary men, untrained, are no match for skilled and experienced armies: "Mere militia who will not submit to rigid discipline cannot be made the equals of regulars by no matter how many years of desultory fighting. In the War of the American Revolution it was the Continentals—the regulars of Washington, Wayne, and Greene—who finally won the victory, while even to the very end of the struggle the ordinary militia proved utterly unable to face the redcoats. So in the English Civil War, it was the carefully drilled and trained horse and foot of the Eastern Association, and not the disorderly London trained bands, who overthrew the king's men. Cromwell had developed his troops just as Grant and Lee, Sherman and Johnson long afterward developed theirs." [68]

Other biographies of Cromwell, no doubt inspired by Thomas Carlyle's reconsideration of Cromwell's life, appeared at the same time as Roosevelt's, so Roosevelt found himself thrown in with John Morley and Charles Firth for review. The professional historians were ruthless: Englishman C. H. Catterall compared the three biographies and thought Roosevelt's courage an effrontery because "his manner of treatment is outgrown." [69] Roosevelt regarded Charles I a tyrant, Bishop Laud a narrow-minded bigot, Thomas Wentworth a renegade, and Cromwell a good man led astray by ambition, according to Catterall, who thought such opinions unscholarly. "His applications of seventeenth-century conditions to present-day affairs in America betray at every step gross ignorance and a lack of real training in the study of history." [70] Apparently Catterall had a rather narrow view of history. On the other hand, the perceptive reviewer for the English review *Antiquary* saw the book differently in his comparison of Roosevelt, Morley, and Firth: "But, apart from the retelling of matter which, as we have said is necessarily common to all these books, this author has found something new to impress upon his readers; and it is really a striking analogy. He finds close analogues for Cromwell, his leaders and the Puritans in the modern history of his own country." [71] The reviewer gives examples of the analogies and concludes, "Mr. Roosevelt is as cautious as he is instructive in his instance of what is really meant by the repetitions of history." [72]

Finally, the *New York Times* of October 6, 1900, provided this evaluation for the general public: "This is one of the most readable books of its kind that has appeared in recent years. There is no dullness in it, and it presents an essentially American appreciation of Cromwell's life and character." [73] Roosevelt does convincingly argue his comparisons. And even if the reader is not persuaded by them, he does reflect upon the comparison of events between the difficult times of English and American history. Roosevelt produced a book of plain, good sense and not a lofty, esoteric, grueling tome that will be replaced by further research.

V   New York *(1891)*

New York was written by Roosevelt in 1890 and was issued by Longmans, Green & Co. as part of the Historical Towns series in 1891 simultaneously in New York and London. The small book cannot qualify as serious history. Roosevelt lists his sources in the first paragraph of his preface; none of them was a primary source and none had been derived from manu-

scripts in Holland, and therefore they furnished limited information on New Amsterdam. Roosevelt acknowledges that his
aim is less to collect new facts than to choose discriminately
from what was available to him and to "show their true meaning
and their relations to one another." [74] His history of New York
mostly avoids the political problems of his own time, although
he did write an additional chapter in 1895 which brought the
book somewhat up to date.

In his first chapter Roosevelt justifies a history of New York:

The history of New York deserves to be studied for more than one
reason. It is the history of the largest English-speaking city which the
English conquered but did not found, and in which though the
English law and governmental system has ever been supreme, yet the
bulk of the population, composed as it is and ever has been of many
shifting strains, has never been English. Again, for the past hundred
years, it is the history of a wonderfully prosperous trading city, the
largest in the world in which the democratic plan has ever been
faithfully tried for so long a time; and the trial, made under some
exceptional advantages and under some exceptional disadvantages, is
of immense interest, alike for the measure in which it has succeeded
and for the measure in which it has failed.[75]

His emphasis on "trading city" continues as he demonstrates
that New York was founded by the New Netherland Company
in 1615 but actually settled by the West India Company in 1621.

Roosevelt then works his way through the Dutch settlements,
the English conquest under James II, the Cromwellian loyalties
that divided New York into aristocrats and popularists, the
black slave revolts, and the events that led to the Revolution.
He concentrates often on religious problems, but his main
emphasis is political. Roosevelt rarely resorts to the certitudes of
his other books. His opinions seem more veiled and more sub-
dued. No flag-waving or sentimentality intrudes on his Revolutionary War discussions. Those who thought of separation formed
a very small knot of republic enthusiasts; the mobs were more
intent upon making life miserable for the Tories; the masses of
the people were content with being inferiors. When the war
came to New York, most of the active patriots left, leaving the
city to Tories and the English army of occupation for seven years.

Roosevelt relates that after the war decisive power passed
from the great Tory families to the small freeholding families.

A state was constructed and New York City became a creature of the state. The city, however, acquired a political prominence which it has never again attained: it was the seat of power of the Federalist party of New York State: "Hamilton, the most brilliant American statesman who ever lived, possessing the loftiest and keenest intellect of his time, was of course easily the foremost champion in the ranks of the New York Federalists; second to him came Jay, pure, strong, and healthy in heart, body, and mind." [76] Hamilton and Jay did all in their power to strengthen the Union. Soon after the presidential election of 1800, New York moved into the camp of the Democratic party and never moved away. The spoils system changed the entire roster of office holders; the influence of the aristocratic "leaven in the loaf" diminished and the "sway of the people was absolute from that time on." [77]

Roosevelt describes life in New York: the atrocious sanitary conditions, the growth of organized charities, the founding of savings banks, the establishment of scientific and literary societies, and the beginning of immigration after the War of 1812.

In 1820 New York contained some 125,000 inhabitants, whose taxpayers and freeholding blacks were eligible to vote two years later. With the opening of the Erie Canal the city grew rapidly. Increasing immigration constantly changed the ethnic character of the city; the Catholic Church began to be important and feared because of its growth. Riots of all sorts, even because of theater presentations, became common. When he notes that twenty rioters were killed by the firing of troops for such mischief, Roosevelt calls the killing "a most salutary and excellent lesson." [78]

Roosevelt also claims some distinction for New York in its helping found a distinctive literature through Washington Irving, James Fenimore Cooper, William Cullen Bryant, and Rodman Drake: "For the first time we had a literature worthy of being so called, which was not saturated with the spirit of servile colonialism, the spirit of humble imitation of things European. Our political life became full and healthy only after we had achieved political independence; and it is quite as true that we never have done and never shall do, anything really worth doing, whether in literature or art, except when working distinctly as Americans." [79] Roosevelt carries this same thesis to social affairs before the Civil War. With the help of the satire of the *Potiphar Papers* (1853) by George William Curtis, Roosevelt chastizes the richer, commercial classes for their obsequious fawning after European travel and aping of Continental manners. He saw no change or progress from the pre–Civil War days of Curtis; the commercial classes chased the dollar so they could copy European amusements.

He covers the period from 1860 to 1890 in a scant thirteen pages, many of these devoted to the draft riots and separatist sympathies of the large Democratic party representation in New York. When he reports that 1,200 rioters were slain by troops, he adds an appositive, "an admirable object-lesson to the remainder." [80] The fashion for riots continued up to 1870.

Roosevelt mentions the Tweed Ring but ignores in the first edition the pervasive corruption of Tammany Hall. He sees the political problems of New York compounded by the ignorance of the immigrant voters, manipulated by self-seeking political mercenaries. However, he is certain and proud of the underlying spirit of patriotism in the city, and the generous fellow-feeling that New Yorkers constantly attain in aiding other sections of the United States when they are struck by catastrophe. He praises the cultural achievements of New York, its theaters, museums, and magazines. General Ulysses S. Grant is especially singled out for residing in New York and for writing his *Memoirs* there—"and it is scarcely too high praise to say that, both because of the intrinsic worth of the matter, and because of its strength and simplicity as a piece of literary work, it almost deserves to rank with the speeches and writings of Abraham Lincoln." [81] (Years later Mark Van Doren agreed with Roosevelt's opinion, calling, in a class lecture at Columbia University, the *Personal Memoirs of Ulysses S. Grant* a neglected American masterpiece.)

Closing his book on his favorite theme of the failure of the unscrupulous rich, Roosevelt regrets that the would-be upper class is based principally on wealth. He believes that the main problem of New York is to assimilate the immigrants. But he is absolutely convinced that New York will always attract people of talent who are seeking careers of unbounded usefulness and interest.

The chapter added in 1895 deals mainly with Tammany Hall and the strange relationship between the saloon-keeper, the politician, and the policeman on the beat. Sketching the work of the Reverend Charles H. Parkhurst, Roosevelt traces the reform movement in New York and the improvements it has produced in its effort to develop clean government in a polyglot community of millions.

Concerning some of Roosevelt's paragraphs the reviewer of the *New York Times* correctly stated, "This intrusion of personal views, however, only adds vigor to his style and imparts to the final chapters and the preface a tone of homily which, though somewhat out of place in a historian, gains by its ingenuousness the reader's good will." [82] The same reviewer concludes, "The main thing is that he has prepared an eminently readable, clear-sighted, and fair treatise on New York, which is none the less enjoyable because it emanates from the mind of a politician (in the good sense) rather than from that of a historian." [83] For a history of New York up to 1895, with persuasive homilies, no better short history of the city can be found today.

VI   *"Men of Action"* (1926)

Hardly qualifying as historical essays, a group of articles and addresses called "Men of Action," comprising about one-half of Volume XI of the *Works*, give Roosevelt's view of certain men of past history, such as Abraham Lincoln, John Marshall, Andrew Jackson, Robert E. Lee, and General Philip H. Sheridan; articles on his contemporaries, including George William Curtis, William McKinley, John Hay, Leonard Wood, Booker T. Washington, Augustus Saint Gaudens, John Muir, Frederick Courteney Selous, and a few others; and even includes items on the settlement of Jamestown, the Louisiana Purchase, the men of the battle of Gettysburg and Antietam, and an address on the American men who died in Cuba during the war.

Much of what Roosevelt says of the historical characters in this collection he expressed elsewhere; however, he never loses his gift of compacting in a short paragraph what might take someone else a page to express:

Throughout his entire life, and especially after he rose to leadership in his party, Lincoln was stirred to his depths by the sense of fealty to a lofty ideal; but throughout his entire life, he also accepted human nature as it is, and worked with keen, practical good sense to achieve results with the instruments at hand. It is impossible to conceive of a man farther removed from baseness, farther removed from corruption, from mere self-seeking; but it is also impossible to conceive of a man of more sane and healthy mind—a man less under the influence of that fantastic diseased morality (so fantastic and diseased as to be in reality profoundly immoral) which makes a man in this workaday world refuse to do what is possible because he cannot accomplish the impossible.[84]

Roosevelt reveals his own greatness of character when he also says of Lincoln:

After long years of iron effort, and of failure that came more often than victory, he at last rose to the leadership of the Republic, at the moment when that leadership had become the stupendous world-task of the time. He grew to know greatness, but never ease. Success came to him, but never happiness, save that which springs from doing well a painful and a vital task. Power was his, but not pleasure. The furrows deepened on his brow, but his eyes were undimmed by either hate or fear. His gaunt shoulders were bowed, but his steel thews never faltered as he bore for a burden the destinies of his people. His great and tender heart shrank from giving pain; and the task allotted to him was to pour out like water the lifeblood of the young men, and to feel in his every fibre the sorrow of the women. Disaster saddened but never dismayed him.[85]

In a mere portion of a sentence he can sum up the story of a man, a fine geologist, privileged to be in the circle of the Henry Adamses, the John Hays—"The Five of Hearts"—and yet who refused the call to greatness:

. . . and, above all, Clarence King, whose friends always pathetically believed that his brilliant and infinitely varied promise would some day take shape in performance.[86]

Sometimes in these essays Roosevelt will utter statements that clarify his positions in other books. One of his preoccupations throughout his writing career was his insistence on the supremacy of the English-speaking race—at best an awkward position because this "race" included Dutch, Irish, German, and undoubtedly, by his understanding, Indian and Negro, so long as the people concerned spoke English and followed the cultural and legal customs derived from the English. In an essay on Joseph Hodges Choate, the outstanding lawyer and diplomat, Roosevelt says that there have been other races as great as the English-speaking people in war, but not in peace. Those great in peace have not been great in war. His point is that only the English-speaking peoples have consistently demonstrated the necessary virtues for both peace and war so "that with the love for letters, with the love of orderly obedience to law, has gone the capacity to stand up stoutly for the right when menaced by any foreign foe." [87]

Indirectly, the most personal of the essays in "Men of Action" is the article he originally wrote for *Outlook* on the death of Frederick Courteney Selous, the African hunter most admired by Roosevelt, and a man who in his sixties insisted on becoming an officer in the British army during World War I to fight the Germans in Africa. Roosevelt respected Selous probably more than any other strenuous type he ever knew. Most of all, he envied Selous his heroic death in battle for his country, a death Roosevelt himself would have preferred to any other.

VII   Hero Tales from American History *(1895)*

Roosevelt collaborated with Henry Cabot Lodge in 1895 to produce *Hero Tales from American History*, stories taken, naturally, from the significant experiences of men in American history. Roosevelt wrote fourteen of the twenty-six stories. Most of the characters are military men, but not all. The tales number from four to seven pages each and, though attempting to avoid didacticism, often do become somewhat preachy. They are effective in their conciseness and will always be useful in educating youth to patriotism and courage. Roosevelt was very much himself when he wrote in one of the tales: "To guard one's own flag against capture is the pride, to capture the flag of one's enemy the ambition, of every valiant soldier." [88]

VIII   *"History as Literature"* (1912)

"History as Literature" represents the finest achievement of Roosevelt's efforts as a historian. Originally the title of a book of his essays published by Charles Scribner's Sons in 1913, it became the first essay in Volume XII of the *Works, Literary Essays*. It was delivered as his annual address when president of the American Historical Association in December 1912. In this essay he urges that the writing of history not be a plodding, dull performance. He recognizes the new scientific bent of history, then stresses the importance of the controlled imagination in writing it. By means of stirring examples, he proceeds to show the uses of the imagination in defining and elaborating his thesis. Of course, history must be scientific, he states; but it also must be literature. In addition, he expects the greatest historian to be a great moralist; however, an obsession with purposeful moral teaching, he warns, can be self-defeating. In the case of Thomas Carlyle's *Frederick the Great* Roosevelt sees literature of a high order, but moral vision obscured and distorted to support Carlyle's own views. Then by way of illustration of his remarks on the use of the imagination in writing history, toward the end of his essay he sketches a thousand years of the history of Russia in one magnificent long paragraph that utilizes all the points of his instruction.

Roosevelt's contribution to the writing of history in this address cannot be overemphasized. Samuel Eliot Morison refers to it on the first page of the *Harvard Guide to American History* and laments that Roosevelt's "trumpet call fell largely on deaf ears, at least in the academic historical profession." [89] The writing of history still sinks under the burden of "long, involved sentences that one has to read two or three times in order to grasp the meaning; poverty in vocabulary, ineptness of expression, weakness in paragraph structure, constant misuse of words and, of late, the introduction of pseudoscientific and psychological jargon." [90] Similarly, in *Allen Nevins on History*, Nevins asks, "What is history?" and answers his own question. "Theodore Roosevelt said that history is a vivid and powerful presentation of scientific matter in literary form; and it would be difficult to improve upon this statement." [91]

How does Roosevelt's own history measure up to his definition in "History as Literature"? Roosevelt appreciated the dichotomy that separated the generalist from the specialist. He saw the weakness of the emphasis on the scientific methodology that led to specialization and an absence of philosophical speculation. The sensitive inclinations of his intelligence emphasized the poetic more than the scientific. As a result, his writing of history is that of the generalist who admits the impact and even the importance of scientific specialization in the writing of history but who prefers to philosophize and leave his personal mark on his work. By the strictest judgment perhaps only *The Winning of the West* could qualify as true history as Roosevelt defines it. The work has all the objective detail Roosevelt could muster. Except for certain Daniel Boone and Davy Crockett materials denied him by L. C. Draper, Roosevelt considered every fragment of data available at the time. Needless to say, the volumes teem with Roosevelt's own philosophical comments. Most important, he brought to the attention of the scholars of the eastern United States the magnificent potentialities of the history of the West. In the instances of the biographies he did not have the resources necessary to fulfill his definition. He wrote *Benton* in the remote frontier near Dickinson, North Dakota; the Morris family papers were denied him; his duties as Governor of New York inhibited his full attention to detail in *Cromwell*. Nevertheless, he still managed to produce his own brand of poetry for each biography—ever the generalist.

The Naval War of 1812 certainly has sufficient scientific qualities to justify its acceptance as true history; however, it should be noted that Roosevelt had the additional task of destroying an antiquated school of defective naval history—that of the British historian William James—and as a consequence Roosevelt permitted his emotional responses to taint his history. But he did succeed in giving the writing of naval history a new methodology, seriousness, and objectivity. These last named characteristics can hardly be expected of *The Rough Riders*. Still he did leave a noble document and resource of the Spanish-American War, superior to any other to come out of that idealistic American enterprise.

New York, the essays in "Men of Action," and *Hero Tales from American History* are more philosophical than scientific, and none remotely qualifies as history, but they boil with the challenge and excitement of imaginative literature. Each of them has the same verve and distance from dullness that Roosevelt sought for not only in others but also in himself.

CHAPTER 3

Author of Outdoor Life

THE one aspect of Theodore Roosevelt's writing which is difficult to represent fairly today is the great number of publications dealing with outdoor life. Many people are horrified at the thought of killing animals in the hunt, and the ways of the early pioneers and ranchers cannot be reconciled with the "civilized" methods of butchering and zoo-keeping that exist in our time. Yet for the pioneer and ranchman of Roosevelt's early years hunting provided the only source of meat, and the careful observation of the large American animals was only just beginning. Moreover, from the first pages of his earliest books on hunting to the last, Roosevelt stressed repeatedly and emphatically the dangers of imminent extinction to various species and the necessity of wildlife conservation.

The principal books of the outdoors which Roosevelt published are *Hunting Trips of a Ranchman* (1885), *Ranch Life and the Hunting Trail* (1888), *The Wilderness Hunter* (1893), *Outdoor Pastimes of an American Hunter* (1905), *A Book-Lover's Holidays in the Open* (1916), *African Game Trails* (1910), and *Through the Brazilian Wilderness* (1914). In addition, various numbers of his papers on natural history have been collected into single volumes. No other American author has surpassed Roosevelt in the diversity of outdoor activity in which he personally participated. He was active on four continents as rancher, hunter, naturalist, or explorer. What is truly remarkable is the meaningfulness of his experiences in terms of his own personal growth. Wherever he went in his travels, something of consequence followed—Theodore Roosevelt and the American people were never the same again. The force of his personality touched all of his adventures, and the exercise of his talent as a writer recorded these developments for all time.

Roosevelt had a solid intellectual foundation for the observation of outdoor life. Despite his poor eyesight, he drilled himself by concentration to be an expert observer of bird life while still a boy. His first manuscripts describe birds; his first mention in an American newspaper by name involved his opinion on birds;[1] his very first printed treatise described the summer birds of the Adirondacks. All of his books give special attention to birds. Wherever he went in the world, they oriented him to the natural life around him; he always made comparisons of the habits and songs of birds he knew with those with which he was newly becoming familiar. While president he provided a comprehensive list of birds observed on the White House grounds.

His earliest attempts at taxidermy required the use of the rifle in collecting specimens. Although never a great expert at target shooting, Roosevelt developed all the skills required by a successful hunter—patience, perseverance, and unlimited courage under pressure. He always expected hunting to be a dangerous pursuit and therefore made no great thing of narrow escapes.

His intellectual capacities for the work of the naturalist and certain philosophical implications associated with such work, despite his disclaimers from time to time, were developed at Harvard. Because he was bored with laboratory work, his career as an academic naturalist ended while he was an undergraduate; nevertheless, his mind was exercised to productive thinking by such teachers as Nathaniel Shaler, the paleontologist, and William James, the noted anatomist and philosopher. Also while at Harvard he was introduced to the geological treatises of James Dwight Dana, the meteorological studies of Alexander Buchan, and books of botany by Asa Gray.[2] He continued his study of James, Darwin, and Herbert Spencer, adopting their views of life's struggles, with severe modifications. As John M. Blum observes: "Roosevelt . . . tempered his Darwinism with inductive conclusions and nonbiological premises and prejudices." [3] In 1884 he was probably the best qualified man in America to take up residence in the West and thereby to make significant contributions to the knowledge of wildlife. When he went to North Dakota, he already knew most of the books published about hunting and the natural history of the West. His book collection on the ranch included Van Dyke's *Still Hunter*, Dodge's *Plains of the Great West*, Caton's *Deer and Antelope of America*, and Coues's *Birds of the Northwest*.

When Roosevelt moved to Medora, North Dakota, the area around the Badlands was undergoing significant changes. He knew that his time was a period of transition. The butcher-hunters had killed off the last of the buffalo herds; cattle were introduced to the area for the first time; the sheep-herders and farmers were gradually moving west. Remnants of recent Indian wars and bitter memories still lingered. Roosevelt was a witness to the disappearance of the old and the arrival of the new.

I Hunting Trips of a Ranchman (1885)

Any mere summary of a book of hunting by Roosevelt will fail to convey adequately what it contains. *Hunting Trips of a Ranchman* begins with a long discourse on ranching, in order to establish in the reader's mind the locale of the hunts. Roosevelt's strong memory and his eye for detail crowd the pages with all kinds of information about life on a northern ranch in 1885: the location of the ranch country, descriptions of ranch facilities and animals, the life of the cowboys, their dress and customs, the changing of the work with the seasons.

The basic context of his story now prepared, Roosevelt begins his chapters on hunting. The first hunts take place around the ranch, and involve a search for birds, notably the hunt for water-fowl. Interestingly, he interrupts his discussion of water-fowl to remark that the extinction of the beaver throughout most of the plains country is a question of but a short time because of over-hunting. He tells of the curlew, the upland or grass plover, and the golden plover for the table; and then in an aside states that no wild beast in the West is as feared as the skunk—it will bite a sleeper and occasionally transmit hydrophobia. (Roosevelt could never restrain himself from telling interesting impressions as they occurred to him.) He continues his colorful stories and observations all through the chapters given separately to the hunts of the grouse of the plains, the canny whitetail deer, the difficult blacktail deer, the sharp-eyed pronghorn or antelope, the almost impossible bighorn or mountain-sheep, the simple buffalo, the stately elk, and finally the dangerous grizzly bear.

In writing *Hunting Trips of a Ranchman*, Roosevelt knew that he was making a unique contribution to outdoor writing; consequently he wanted to avoid the mere recitation of kills that stigmatized almost all of the hunting books published at that time. He sought to describe hunting but also to introduce at every possible occasion information about the life of the animals which he was hunting, to describe the terrain, and to comment on life in the West. Roosevelt not only describes the life around the Little Missouri River, he gives unrestrained opinions on everything that he mentions: Texans are the best cowboys; the best horses are from Oregon; a wolf will never attack a man; the unbounded freedom of ranch life will disappear, diminished to oblivion by the fences of grangers; skin-hunters and meat-hunters cannot vanish soon enough. Sometimes his opinions go beyond the immediacy of his concerns and become reflective, as when he comments that the Indians really had no more claim to the land than anyone else because they merely kept moving, like transients, to where the game was plentiful, moving out weaker rivals to the claimed area until they themselves were displaced by even stronger rivals. Still, he would have everyone treated the same, including the Indians. Everyone is entitled to a homestead, even if it means the destruction of the cattle industry, which end he sees as inevitable. The people who work the land, who intend to stay on it, are the real owners—not the transients or profit makers. Roosevelt did not write *Hunting Trips of a Ranchman* only to tell of successful hunts; the emphasis in his book resides in "Ranchman" as well, for it is the ranch that is his underlying concern.

He loved the life of the rancher; the robust life came to mean everything to him. He looked with disdain on anyone who would choose an easier way of life. For example, he witnessed the growth of the sheep herds, and his judgment of the men who owned them was severe: "The sheep-herders are a morose, melancholy set of men, generally afoot, and with no companionship except that of the bleating idiots they are hired to guard. No man can associate with sheep and retain his self-respect. Intellectually, a sheep is about on the lowest level of the brute creation; why the early Christians admired it, whether young or old, is to a good cattleman always a profound mystery." [4] Roosevelt really had more respect for some animals than he did for some men, but he sentimentalized over neither men or animals. He came to revere the challenge of cold and storm. A night in a wet blanket he accepted philosophically, even though he didn't relish it.

What is especially noteworthy in his commentary is his acceptance of change. Although he regretted the passing of the old freedom of the range, he regretted even more the destruction of the buffalo. Yet they had to go: the horse, the long-range rifle, and the coming of the cattle doomed them. He writes mournfully that the species, in terms of huge herds roaming from Pennsylvania to the Rockies, is all but extinct, and then comments that the buffalo could survive only if the land remained sparsely settled: "Its destruction was the condition precedent upon the advance of white civilization in the West, and was a positive boon to the more thrifty and industrious frontiersman. Where the buffalo were plenty, they ate up all the grass that could have supported cattle." [5] He adds that the extermination of the buffalo was the inevitable solution of the Indian question, because the Indian could no longer leave the reservation and be sure of an ample supply of meat to support him in the event of war.

Contemporary notices of *Hunting Trips of a Ranchman* were quite favorable. The book was issued first in the Medora edition of 500 elaborately bound copies. The *Spectator* of January 16, 1886, reviewed it with praise, although the reviewer at first had some apprehensions, being appalled that a book on hunting would be bound at such expense and with such good taste. However, the reviewer immediately acknowledges that despite his fears, the book was not just "the chronicles of revolting butchery" usually found in hunting books; assuredly, the hunting episodes are merely the pegs or skeletons on which the lover of nature could hang his observations: "What Bret Harte has done for the miners Theodore Roosevelt has done for the more manlier and useful folk of the plains, the ranchmen and cowboys." [6]

Forest and Stream also appreciated the freshness of Roosevelt's book and stated that not long before its appearance "a man who went gunnin' or fishin' lost caste among respectable people just about in the same way that one did who got drunk." [7] The reviewer, later identified as George Bird Grinnell, the great naturalist and editor of *Forest and Stream*, found fault with some hunting myths offered as fact, and was especially disappointed with some of the poor illustrations of elk. The book had been illustrated by artists of the time, including A. B. Frost, R. Swain Gifford, J. C. Beard, Fannie E. Gifford, and Henry Sandham. The criticism was not wasted on the author. The odious illustrations were dropped in subsequent editions. At the first opportunity Roosevelt visited Grinnell, and the two became colleagues in working for the conservation of wildlife resources.

In its review, the *New York Times* generously summarized

most of the book, pointing out helpful information generally unknown in the East and concluded, "Mr. Roosevelt writes most
happily, tells naturally what he sees and does, and 'Hunting
Trips of a Ranchman' will take a leading position in the literature
of the American sportsman." [8]

As the reviewers perceived, *Hunting Trips of a Ranchman*
remains much more than a study of hunting trips; it tells of the
sage-cock, the rattlesnake, the horned frog, the prairie-dog,
quicksand on a dry prairie, and the whole natural world of long
ago. In his discussion of the elk, Roosevelt tells of its gradual
extinction at the hands of "Man the Destroyer," its only effective
enemy. Roosevelt had hunted elk in Montana and Wyoming,
taking a pack-train on a fortnight's journey. The reader knows
everything there is to know about pack-trains in a few pages.
When Roosevelt gets to the elk country, he gives some of his best
descriptions of a country where no man ever stepped before. His
survival depends upon his best woodsman's skills. How simple
it could be to pick the wrong ridge or water course back to the
horses. The weather is always cold; snow falls; but he is cozy in
an improvised tent among the pines and spruces with his "small
supply of books for just such occasions." He ends the chapter by
telling of the great satisfaction of returning with the mighty
antlers that serve as a trophy and proof of successful skill in
sport. Anyone who likes hiking and camping will know that
Roosevelt saw outdoor life at its best.

Today, *Hunting Trips of a Ranchman* will have lost very little
of its appeal to anyone interested in life on a North Dakota ranch
in the 1880s. The hunting of the various animals may appeal to
hunters, but the observations Roosevelt recorded should interest
the natural historians who wish to know the habits of animals in
locations now lost to them. Roosevelt insists constantly that
animals change habits when exposed to man. He explains convincingly the glorious freedom of movement that he experienced,
the surprises, the frustrations, always with sufficient objectivity.
He knows the art of keeping alive suspense until the end of the
chase. The ordinary reader with some aversion to hunting is won
over to his stories and adventures because his observations and
comments never stop. He tells precisely why he feels that the
blacktail cannot survive the encroachment of man, whereas the
whitetail can. He constantly matches the resources of the animals
with those of the hunter, giving each species its rating for eye-

sight, wariness, agility, and courage. No such book could be written today; that world is gone. Roosevelt's hunting trips, given the circumstances of his time, cannot be considered an abomination or a perversion. His writing is forthright, deliberate, objective. He does not romanticize his pursuits. His purpose is to describe and to present information.

II   Ranch Life and the Hunting Trail *(1888)*

In 1888 Roosevelt wrote a series of articles for the *Century Magazine* which were collected later in the year to appear as *Ranch Life and the Hunting Trail*. The volume was profusely illustrated by Frederic Remington. Sixty-four illustrations used in the magazine articles were increased to eighty-two for the book. Even though a great body of American literature has chronicled ranch life in the West, very little of it touches North Dakota as does Roosevelt's.

The articles from *Century Magazine* were arranged so that "The Cattle Country of the Far West" commences the volume. Roosevelt gives an overview of all the cattle country of the West, from the Rio Grande to the Canadian border—open range, and hardly a farm; "Cowboys and branding-irons take the place of fences." [9] Roosevelt concentrates his descriptions on the region of the Little Missouri River. He begins by telling how to find a suitable range for the cattle, and how to create a rough camp and then a ranch—probably twenty miles from the next ranch. Visitors are rare: "Parties of hunters and trappers call now and then. Most rarely small bands of emigrants go by in search of new homes, impelled by the restless, aimless craving for change so deeply grafted in the breast of the American borderer: the white-topped wagons are loaded with domestic goods, with sallow, dispirited-looking women, and with tow-headed children; while the gaunt, moody frontiersmen slouch alongside, rifle on shoulder, lank, homely, uncouth, and yet with a curious suggestion of grim strength underlying it all. Or cowboys from neighboring ranches will ride over, looking for lost horses or seeing if their cattle have strayed off the range. But this is all. Civilization seems as remote as if we were living in an age long past." [10]

This land will give nothing for nothing; "now and then miserable farmers straggle in to fight a losing and desperate battle with drought, cold, and grasshoppers." [11] Even today dump holes contain the remnants of their rusted equipment in barren stretches between the buttes. A few "cow towns" survived to become like Miles City. Roosevelt transmits the color of such towns with their wooden sidewalks and cheap-looking board houses, the hunters from the plains and mountains, the surly teamsters, the trappers, the wolfers, and gaunt Indians. No detail escapes Roosevelt's fancy and delight. He knew men; and when he talks of the buffalo-hunters, the reader must believe him:

The old buffalo-hunters, who formed a distinct class, became powerful forces for evil once they had destroyed the vast herds of mighty beasts the pursuit of which had been their means of livelihood. They were absolutely shiftless and improvident; they had no settled habits; they were inured to peril and hardship, but entirely unaccustomed to steady work; and so they afforded just the materials from which to make the bolder and more desperate kinds of criminals. When the game was gone they hung round the settlements for some little time, and then many of them naturally took to horse-stealing, cattle-killing, and highway robbery, although others, of course, went into honest pursuits. They were men who died off rapidly, however; for it is curious to see how many of these plainsmen, in spite of their iron nerves and thews, have their constitutions completely undermined, as much by the terrible hardships they have endured as by the fits of prolonged and bestial revelry with which they have varied them.[12]

In this same first chapter Roosevelt follows with a description of the "bad men," or professional fighters. Roosevelt had respect for them and their skills and bravery, but he adds, "These desperados always try to 'get the drop' on a foe—that is, to take him at a disadvantage before he can use his own weapon. I have known more men killed in this way, when the affair was wholly one-sided, than I have known to be shot in a fair fight; and I have known fully as many who were shot by accident. It is wonderful, in the event of a street fight, how few bullets seem to hit the men they are aimed at." [13] Lynch law or the law of the vigilantes existed in Roosevelt's time, as well; one committee in eastern Montana during one short reform period hanged nearly sixty horse and cattle thieves.

The second chapter, "Out on the Range," recites the life of the rough-rider of the plains, the hero of rope and revolver. The methods and equipment of the Spanish ranches moved gradually north; even the vocabulary is borrowed from the Mexicans. In one

paragraph Roosevelt gives a complete description of the use of
the rope. Riding follows, almost as if of lesser importance; brand-
ing next; and then the range is described. No text could be more
complete. The perils are rendered in awful detail; for example:

Again, the grass is, of course, soonest eaten off where there is shelter;
and accordingly, the broken ground to which the animals cling during
winter may be grazed bare of vegetation though the open plains, to
which only the hardiest will at this season stray, may have plenty;
and insufficiency of food, although not such as actually to starve them,
weakens them so that they succumb readily to the cold or to one of
the numerous accidents to which they are liable—as slipping off an
icy butte or getting cast in a frozen washout. The cows in calf are
those that suffer most, and so heavy is the loss among these and so
light the calf crop that it is yet an open question whether our northern
ranges are as a whole fitted for breeding. When the animals get weak
they will huddle into some nook or corrner and simply stay there till
they die. An empty hut, for instance, will often in the spring be found
to contain the carcasses of a dozen weak cows or poor steers that have
crawled into it for protection from the cold and, once in, have never
moved out.[14]

Overstocking also produces extensive loss. How can it be
controlled? Prophetically, Roosevelt concludes that stock-raising
in that form is doomed and will hardly outlast the century: The
great free ranches will pass away before the onward march of our
people; very few to come later will ever see "what is perhaps the
pleasantest, healthiest, and most exciting phase of American
existence." [15]

The chapter on "The Home-Ranch" conveys much of his own
comfortable style of living; but it also, again, tells of the work and
perils of ranching. A horse will return 200 miles to its old haunts;
some horses will stray for a year or eighteen months. A rider can
get lost on a dark night if he doesn't return with the remaining
daylight. The tasks on the ranch are endless; most of them pertain
to the breaking and care of horses. Roosevelt's narratives supply
the best portions of his work, as when he describes the battle
between two horses and a jackass.

If Roosevelt has one gift greater than that of writing narrative,
it is telling of the birds, of which he was uncommonly aware. In
his chapter on the home-ranch, he gives expert descriptions of
the birds of North Dakota and cites individual experiences with

them and their songs. This subject provokes him to further nature observations of the prairie-dog, the skunk, and other small species.

Since this is a book of ranch life, "The Round-up" of springtime merits a special chapter. This event of six weeks' duration is full of excitement. The horses, such as Macaulay, Wire Fence, Dynamite Jimmy, Water Skip, and Fall Back, all have to be reconditioned for their tasks. A hundred thousand miles of land is mapped into round-up districts. The captain of the round-up arranges a meeting place. Every ranch sends its twelve or so cowboys and four-horse wagons. Tender horses with rough habits require more than ordinary riders. Roosevelt on his first round-up was treated unmercifully by his nine horses; he suffered a broken rib by one, and a damaged shoulder by another. Many other riders suffered even worse. Some cowboys are killed every year. Roosevelt writes with unfeigned resoluteness about these risks and injuries, and suddenly the reader realizes that this is a world of men; women are never mentioned, except for the one who later makes Roosevelt a buckskin shirt.

Roosevelt describes the kind of men that constitute the round-up. The cowboys are a breed apart, and the world will never see their like again. They lived by their own code: "Meanness, cowardice, and dishonesty are not tolerated. There is a high regard for truthfulness and keeping one's word, intense contempt for any kind of hypocrisy, and a hearty dislike for a man who shirks his work." [16]

As Roosevelt continues his story of the round-up, it assumes a grandeur of epic proportions. It is no wonder such a scene has provided Hollywood with unlimited opportunities. The wranglers, the cooks, the foremen are small compared to the enormity of the range to be covered and the gigantic herds collected. Fifteen miles at a time comprise an average daily assignment to work. Every page transmits information carrying the force of eyewitness. Finally, the cutting out of individual animals from the herd begins. This specialty requires the best horses and the best riders. The quicker each ranch gets its own cattle, the quicker the round-up concludes. Each ranch takes its own cattle, brands the young, and returns home. In its excitement and adventure lie more seeds of The Strenuous Life, Roosevelt's philosophy of life and action.

"Winter Weather" also deservedly becomes a special chapter.

Waiting out a storm requires patience; once while waiting out a storm, Roosevelt read *Hamlet* to a Texan cowboy and relished his shrewd comments. No one ventures out unless it is absolutely necessary. Landmarks disappear; all signs of life disappear. The whole earth is granite. Many cattle die of starvation.

Roosevelt reaches the fullness of his powers of observation and writing in his chapter on "Frontier Types" in *Ranch Life and the Hunting Trail*. He arrived in North Dakota just when the old hunters and trappers were dying out, but he knew some of them, and he heard their tales. Roosevelt's cattle were among the first to supplant the hunting grounds. He recognized the hunter as the last archetype of freedom, dependent on no one. Some were men of courage and integrity; some were not:

I had with me at the time a hunter who, though their equal as marksman or woodsman, was their exact opposite morally. He was a pleasant companion and useful assistant, being very hard-working and possessing a temper that was never ruffled by anything. He was also a good-looking fellow, with honest brown eyes; but he no more knew the difference between right and wrong than Adam did before the fall. Had he been at all conscious of his wickedness, or had he possessed the least sense of shame, he would have been unbearable as a companion; but he was so perfectly pleasant and easy, so good-humoredly tolerant of virtue in others, and he so wholly lacked even a glimmering suspicion that murder, theft, and adultery were matters of anything more than individual taste, that I actually grew to be rather fond of him.[17]

While a government scout, this same fellow had bought cartridges from army troops at a cent apiece and sold them to the warring Apaches for a dollar. This man and other characters whom Roosevelt describes rival, as life often does, the fictional creations of a Jack London. Roosevelt tells the story of two hunters driven by hunger to stalk one another for the meager portion of flour that each carried. He explains the plight of cowboys running from the law of Texas. Roosevelt touches upon everything around Medora from horseplay to horse thieves. Usually the men who are shot to death, he declares, deserved what they got. He relates a shooting which he says was also chronicled by Bret Harte for the local paper, the *Bad Lands Cowboy*: Welshy shot Hay; the bullet went along Hay's breastbone, into his body, out at the shoulder, and fell into his hand; Hay went up to Welshy and said, "Here, man, here's the bullet." [18]

At this point in his book Roosevelt talks of the hard lot of women on the frontier, beauty and bloom gone from them before their youth. He tells of the woman who made his buckskin shirt as being necessarily resourceful, "having dismissed her husband six months previously in an exceedingly summary manner." [19] Just when Roosevelt arrives at her door, he meets three Sioux who had just caught a white man who had stolen a horse from them. The woman wouldn't care one bit if they hanged the man, saying that red thieves and white thieves deserved the same fate. Her sense of justice and fairness so appealed to Roosevelt that he was willing to make her sheriff and Indian agent for the territory.

To inform the reader on the status of the Indians, Roosevelt includes a chapter called "Red and White on the Border." On his ranch he has a firm policy of treating Indians as fairly as if they were whites. Roosevelt knew that some young Indians could be truculent, insolent, and reckless, and was careful when he met such alone on the plains. On one occasion he was charged by a small group of Indians. As soon as he drew a bead on one, they all halted. Roosevelt would not let any one of them come closer than fifty yards. Eventually, he led his horse away from the area without further incident. He then explains why a few cool whites can beat back larger bands of Indians, the whites' style of combat being more dependable than that of firing from a running horse.

As in all his writing, Roosevelt tries to be fair in placing blame for the terrible relations between reds and whites. Atrocities abound on both sides. He attributes most difficulty for one race blaming all of another race for the actions of one or a few. He also is impatient with those who overlook crimes against anyone of a different race, red or white. He had fixed opinions on Indians and considered them as follows:

Not only do Indians differ individually, but they differ as tribes. An upper-class Cherokee is nowadays as good as a white. The Nez Percés differ from the Apaches as much as a Scotch laird does from a Calabrian bandit. A Cheyenne warrior is one of the most redoubtable foes in the whole world; a "digger" Snake one of the most despicable. The Pueblo is as thrifty, industrious, and peaceful as any European peasant, and no Arab of the Soudan is a lazier, wilder robber than is the Arapahoe.[20]

In the fewest words Roosevelt tells of incident after incident that project the utter confusion of life for reds and whites living together. Yet he also carefully points to incidents of successful intermarriage. A sense of fairness pervades his chapter in the face of an impossible, fluid existence for both races.

Roosevelt was proud of his work as a deputy sheriff, and devotes a chapter to such work. This chapter describes an event also related in his *Autobiography*. A boat he used for crossing the river to get to his horses was stolen, as evidenced by a cut rope. The men of the ranch had a fair idea who had stolen the boat and gone downstream—three hard characters from twenty miles north, already suspected of other crimes. Two of Roosevelt's cowboys, Seawall and Dow, former Maine woodcraftsmen, quickly built a flat-bottom craft for the pursuit. Roosevelt and the two gathered supplies and began the chase three days later. Passage was not easy through the ice packs and ice walls. They shot prairie-fowl for meat as they progressed. The days grew colder. They then were able to shoot some deer to be certain of provisions during the pursuit. In the middle of the third day they caught one of the thieves, unaware, at his campsite. Later, the other two returned and were easily taken. The journey back with the captives was no easy task because of the cold. Among other problems, the captives could not be tied for fear of freezing their hands. Roosevelt, Seawall, and Dow took turns by a huge evening fire as guards. They continued downstream for eight more days, slowly following ice jams. Roosevelt contented himself by reading *Anna Karenina* in gray surroundings that harmonized with Tolstoy. Eventually they reached the cow camp of a ranch, and thus transportation. Roosevelt took the thieves by wagon to Dickinson, remaining awake for thirty-six hours.

The remaining chapters of the book fit the second half of the title, and cover subjects already touched upon in *Hunting Trips of a Ranchman*. There is first a chapter on the use of the rifle in hunting various species, especially the antelope. Their superior eyesight, for example, makes them a formidable quarry. This chapter is actually a summary of all kinds of hunting with the rifle, even that using dogs.

A chapter on an elk-hunt for provisions and a chapter on the bighorn sheep convey significant amounts of information about these species. The last chapter narrates a trip to the mountains of Montana. Again Roosevelt tells of regions never visited before by any man. This time he runs over mountains in vain to bag a white mountain goat. Very few men would be capable of such a pursuit, and even fewer would even think of trying it. Roosevelt explains that nerve, daring, and physical hardihood must be available for the hunt of mountain game. He proves his point convincingly when at last he bags two mountain goats on the trip: he makes no claim for marksmanship, only for patience and perseverance.

What does Roosevelt accomplish in *Ranch Life and the Hunting Trail?* For one thing he has left a living, vibrant, eye-witness account of the life of the ranchers and people of North Dakota. What is more, he has revealed much about himself as a vigorous, enthusiastic young man from the East, competent to take on tasks wholly foreign to him and to transmit his experiences with veracity and photographic conviction.

This book is unique among Roosevelt's outdoor writing—or all of his books, for that matter—in that it concentrates on character. Roosevelt knew men well, and in *Ranch Life and the Hunting Trail* may be found his most extensive analyses of human beings. He was not in the least a prude, nor did he have any trace of superiority toward the humble, forgotten people around him. Each person whom Roosevelt describes becomes the most important person at the moment Roosevelt is writing about him. Without realizing it at the time, Roosevelt was training himself for the presidency. He accepted all people from all walks of life and tried always to see the good in them. Yet he also did not hesitate to castigate the malicious. Character after character comes to life on his pages. Regrettably, Roosevelt never concentrated so clearly on vignettes of character in his later books. Only occasionally did he stop to present a person as a very particular character; however, when he does, the same amusing and caring attitude tells us as much about Roosevelt as about the person on the page.

III   The Wilderness Hunter *(1893)*

The Wilderness Hunter was first issued by G. P. Putnam's Sons in 1893. The book is an attempt to present material not used in his previous two books of hunting, and is based on field notes he typically kept on his excursions. He first describes in capsule form the movement west from the Atlantic settlements, and then begins a description of the game to be found across the country

around 1890. A series of chapters on hunting particular species
follows his historical survey: the blacktail deer, the pronghorn
antelope, the bighorn sheep, the white goat, the caribou, the
round-horned elk, the moose, the bison, the black bear, the grizzly bear, the cougar, and the peccary. Four final chapters
describe hunting with dogs, particularly for the wolf, and life in
the West.

Before the publication of this book, Roosevelt helped to form
the Boone and Crockett Club for the purpose of wildlife conservation. One of the great merits of *The Wilderness Hunter* is its
demonstrating that the author is just as interested in live animals
as in dead ones. In bare outline the book seems to be a list of
killings; but it is much more. The surroundings of the animals,
their habits, their feeding, their means of survival, and their
perilous existence are described in the manner of the trained
naturalist. If one is a hunter, here for him is a complete course
in the hunting of great game; if one is not, there still is available
an encylopedic survey of animals, birds, flowers, and trees in their
natural terrain.

These hunting stories would be as repetitious a recitation of
kills and chases as many others, however, were it not for Roosevelt's customary digressions. The most interesting of them are
like those of his previous books dealing with Western characters.
In describing a prongbuck hunt, he stops to tell of a visit to an
old hunter, and the man comes to life as quickly on the page as
would a character on a page in one of Charles Dickens's books.
Roosevelt once said that he did not have the gifts of a novelist,
yet his characters and stories carry the conviction of the best
realism. His descriptions of action can be exemplified best in his
tale of a prairie fire which comes in the prongbuck chapter. The
urgency of the moment involves the saving of winter feed. As
soon as night comes and the wind diminishes, the party shoot a
steer and split the carcass in two, lengthwise, with an axe. Then
two riders, one of them Roosevelt, drag a half-carcass, bloody
side down, with ropes to the fore and hind legs, over the snakes
of flame. The other men follow on foot with slickers and wet
saddle blankets. The weight of the half-carcass and its moisture
smother the fire; the two men following behind beat out any
isolated tufts of flame. The confusion in that night rivals any
adventure of western ranching.

The best chapter in Roosevelt's book is undoubtedly the one titled "In Cowboy Land." Here he tries to explain the morality and the law of people living in elemental conditions. The transformation from rude virtue to civilized behavior by means of law does not suggest that the earlier types were without their good sides. Roosevelt believes that the westerners were certainly as good as the Normans in the days of the battle of Hastings, and probably superior in ethics and morality to the Vikings of the years before Hastings. In this chapter he tells two stories, one that he heard, one that he experienced. He had more than ordinary talent in the use of dialogue; however, these stories are rare instances of his rendering narrative with extensive dialogue. One of them, for example, concerns a man seeking justice against another man for stealing a horse. The judge has a peculiar sense of justice because he tells the injured man to shoot the thief when he returns to his home. The wronged man has second thoughts while waiting in ambush; he may by mistake shoot another man visiting the thief's wife. Roosevelt's sense of humor fits in well with the tradition in the West delineated so well by Constance Rourke in *American Humor*. What else can one do in the face of injustice by stupid animals, contrary humans, savages, and the elements except laugh or go mad? As one story follows another, the reader can sense the kind of companionship that Roosevelt would offer in a land where storytelling was the main source of entertainment. The stories of the chase for animals may become tedious after a time, but the constant flow of natural history and the descriptions of the people hold the attention.

The last chapter of *The Wilderness Hunter* surveys the hunting opportunities throughout the West. Roosevelt admires the stalwart democracy that the lonely life of the wilderness offers to any who want it. He urges those who go into the wilds to be aware of all the sights and sounds. He urges all to read the works of John Burroughs: "As a woodland writer, Thoreau comes second only to Burroughs." [21] Roosevelt recommends Audubon, Coues, Bendire, Hart Merriam, Maurice Thompson, and Oliver Thorne Miller. He states that few good hunting books exist: Caton's *Deer and Antelope in America*, Van Dyke's *Still Hunter*, Elliott's *Carolina Sports*, and Dodge's *Hunting Grounds of the Great West*. He also admires Clarence King for his classic *Mountaineering In The Sierra Nevada*, Francis Parkman for his

Oregon Trail, Washington Irving for his *Tour of the Prairies,* and
James Fenimore Cooper for his novels. These men were among
the greatest stylists who wrote of the West, and no doubt influenced Roosevelt considerably in his ambitions for his own
writing. He closes the book with verbatim quotations from diaries
of fishing and hunting by Daniel Webster and George Washington, the latter's writing as direct and objective as Roosevelt's own.

The *New York Times* found a healthy Americanism in Roosevelt's *Wilderness Hunter:* "Mr. Roosevelt's Americanism shows
itself in the very beginning in the two quotations from Whitman
and Joaquin Miller, which he has selected as mottoes, and in his
preface he expresses the opinion that the possession of no other
qualities by a nation can atone for the lack of that vigorous
manliness which the chase cultivates." [22] The reviewer goes on
to state that "there is not a trace of vainglory in Mr. Roosevelt's
account of his hunting adventures." [23] The book is recommended
for all those going to the West or anyone wanting to know more
of that part of the American wilderness. The reviewer would have
understood even better Roosevelt's stressing Americanism and
manliness if he had known that Roosevelt was hard at work on
his *The Winning of the West* at the same time that he was writing
The Wilderness Hunter. The task of the pioneer required the
same virtues as those of the daring hunter; in the eyes of Roosevelt, the achievements of the early hunters, followed by the
pioneers, are what made America.

A very favorable review of *The Wilderness Hunter* by J. H.
Porter appeared in the *Atlantic Monthly.* Porter very astutely
points out that men involuntarily reveal much of themselves in
writing such books and continues: "Mr. Roosevelt makes no display of scientific attainments, rarely refers to authorities, never
indulges in theoretical disquisitions upon the many and strikingly
contrasted creatures with which he came in contact. He tells us
what he knows of them, nothing more; but this is done so fully,
so fairly, and with so complete an absence of preconception,
prejudice, and errors attributable to the sources just pointed out,
that it is merely a plain statement of the truth to say of this book
that it stands nearly alone in the literature of sport with large
game." [24] Porter concludes that nothing so thorough and satis-
factory concerning grizzly bears had yet appeared, and considers
this essay and that in Roosevelt's *Ranch Life and the Hunting
Trail* the best available about these animals at that time.

IV   Outdoor Pastimes of an American Hunter *(1905)*

Outdoor Pastimes of an American Hunter opens with a chapter describing a hunt for cougar in the Colorado Rockies in 1901. The success of the hunt depends upon the hunting hounds, how well trained they are, how valiant. Roosevelt offers considerable detail concerning the keeping of such hounds, the habits of cougars, and the hunting of bobcats as well. The next chapter gives the details of a bear-hunt in 1905, his first bear-hunt with hounds. His digressions on birds, small animals, and the prowess of dogs make the chapter more than a mere hunting yarn. The same year Roosevelt hunted coyotes or prairie wolves, and these hunts provide the material for "Wolf-Coursing." A man who captures these beasts, Abernathy by name, fascinates Roosevelt, who gives a detailed explanation of the man's technique. A return to the hunting of prongbuck in the next chapter is a nostalgic journey back to the days of ranching. Four more chapters tell of mountain-sheep, whitetail deer, blacktail deer, and the elk—subjects he covered previously in other books. A chapter on "Wilderness Reserves: The Yellowstone Park" offers some of Roosevelt's strong arguments in favor of conservation, which he saw as "essentially a democratic movement" for preserving the beautiful reserves for all the people, not just for rich sportsmen. He tells in some detail of a visit to Yellowstone Park with John Burroughs, the eminent naturalist.

The most comprehensive and scholarly essay in the book is "Books on Big Game." This chapter amounts to a short history of hunting in Western Civilization. Roosevelt acts as critic in reviewing well-known books on hunting. His requirements for approval consist mainly in that the books on hunting be interesting, certainly more than mere itineraries. It is apparent that Roosevelt looks for information about the lives of the animals as much as the hunting of them. Game-butchery never interested him.

When Roosevelt speaks of birds, he is at his best. "At Home" is a chapter describing his fascination with the birds of Long Island and Washington, D.C. He also describes domesticated animals that came into the circle of his family. "In the Louisiana Cane-Brakes," a series of hunts for deer and bear, and "Small Country Neighbors," information on small animals and birds, complete the book.

Roosevelt was President of the United States when he published *Outdoor Pastimes of an American Hunter*. Its contents were drawn from his articles in *Scribner's Magazine* and from various pieces he had written for the Boone and Crockett Club publications. He dedicated the book to John Burroughs. The *Harvard Graduates' Magazine* of March 1905 considered the book to be the "most entertaining he has ever produced," complimented Roosevelt on the veracity and fluency of his words, and concluded, "He is never dull in his matter nor inopportune in his digressions." [25] These comments may be true for those who have not read his earlier books. Actually, Roosevelt is somewhat repetitious here, and an alert reader can detect that these essays were dictated rather than written. As a consequence they are not as tightly knit as were his earlier hunting books. In one paragraph he tells of bobcats being fond of prairie-dogs and haunting the dog-towns in spring. Four sentences later he begins a paragraph with bobcats being fond of prairie-dog-towns and lurking around them in the spring. The enormous inundation of facts, stories, digressions, and fascinating details about wolves, dogs, grizzlies, weasels, deer, and birds never ceases. Roosevelt keeps verbal track of almost all of the twenty-six hounds and four terriers on a chase, and in the next moment has the reader with him hanging over a cliff, held by the legs, so that Roosevelt can shoot a cougar. The details and stories are exhausting, but of their sort there can be none superior in the rendering of such unflinching enthusiasm.

For the general reader Roosevelt's chapter on hunting books, "Books on Big Game," should prove most engrossing. Proud of his own library, he surveys the field of hunting from the time of the Assyrians and Alexander the Great, through the Middle Ages in Europe, to the American settlers and Buffalo Bill. He considers most of the multitude of hunting books to be bad, just as most novels and poems are bad. He regrets that no truly great writer of the hunt has yet appeared. His belief is that only the big-game hunter could really know these animals. An "anaemic" Thoreau or a Burroughs limiting his wanderings to the Potomac or the Hudson could never have felt the beat of hardy life in his veins, or he would have charged off to the Rocky Mountains and abandoned the homelier and less grandiose side of nature. What Roosevelt demands is what he himself tried to do: "Not only should the hunter be able to describe vividly the chase and the life habits of the quarry, but he should also draw the wilderness itself and the life of those who dwell or sojourn therein. We wish to see before us the cautious stalk and the headlong gallop; the great beasts as they feed or rest or run or make love or fight; the wild hunting camps; the endless plains shimmering in the sunlight; the vast, solemn forests; the desert and the marsh and the mountain chain; and all that lies hidden in the lonely lands through which the wilderness wanderer roams and hunts game." [26] He abhors the thought of "fine writing" as inappropriate for such a subject, but he wants more than the usual recitation of an itinerary which is as dull as a cookbook.

In this chapter on the books of big game, Roosevelt shows his best traits of survey and judgment. It probably stands as the finest short essay on this topic ever written. True, it will never claim a huge audience; nevertheless, it neatly outlines all that can be said of an activity that, historically, made possible the survival of the human species. Men were hunters before they were farmers. Roosevelt chose to believe that the virtues of the hunter were the reservoirs of the virtues needed for men willing to defend this country: "No nation facing the unhealthy softening and relaxation of fibre which tend to accompany civilization can afford to neglect anything that will develop hardihood, resolution, and the scorn of discomfort and danger. But if sport is made an end instead of a means, it is better to avoid it altogether." [27]

V   African Game Trails *(1910)*

If Roosevelt had visited the Happy Hunting Grounds of the American Indians and then returned to life, he could not have had more satisfying hunts than those of the *African Game Trails*. He considered this trip to British East Africa a return to the Pleistocene Age, with its abundance of huge animals. Moreover, even though he himself was growing tired of killing animals, scientific justification impelled him to lead this expedition on behalf of the National Museum at Washington, the American Museum of Natural History in New York, and the National Collection of Heads and Horns at the Bronx Zoological Gardens. In 1910 very little was known in America of the species of mammals, birds, reptiles, and plants of Africa. By the time Roosevelt finished, the museums of the United States had some of the best collections in the world. [28]

In the first chapter of *African Game Trials* Roosevelt notes that he sailed on March 23, 1909, in order to lead a scientific expedition in Africa authorized by the Smithsonian Institute for the purpose of collecting specimens for the National Museum. Accompanied by his son Kermit, an undergraduate at Harvard, and by three naturalists, Edgar A. Mearns, Edmund Heller, and J. Alden Loring, Roosevelt had fully prepared for the expedition. Widespread interest in his scientific venture was attested by the gift of an elephant gun from fifty-six of the most noted zoologists, sportsmen, and authors in the world. Roosevelt and his party sailed on the *Hamburg*, changed to the *Admiral* at Naples, passed through the Suez Canal, and on April 21 reached Mombasa in British East Africa (modern Kenya). In the Azores and at Aden, at the southern tip of the Red Sea, the naturalists had already begun en route their collecting of specimens. The train ride to Nairobi Roosevelt describes as, for natural historians, the most interesting railway journey in the world. The English had already marked off huge game reserves for intelligent game preservation, to which Roosevelt devotes pages of gratitude for their actions and admiration of the wonders about him—hartbeests, monkeys, giraffes, ostriches, and countless other species.

Eventually they set up camp on the Kapiti plains, where Roosevelt meets the native guides and bearers for the safari as well as the European hunters who will accompany his party. Their plan will lead them in a generally northwest direction to Lake Victoria, then more northerly into Uganda, and finally directly north through the Congo and Sudan. There were many side journeys throughout the safari: visits to ranches in Kitanga, to the plains of the Guaso Nyero, and the Uasin Gishu Plateau. Roosevelt devotes separate chapters to lion hunting, the gathering of specimens of rhinoceros and giraffe, the pursuit of hippopotamus and leopard, the stalking of the dangerous African buffalo, and finally the killing of elephants.

African Game Trails defies any brief summary. As George Bird Grinnell explained in his review of the book, it covers much more than the title suggests or the summary indicates. The title suggests only a mere hunting story; and although the hunting yarns are interesting and truly exciting, they are only a small part. The essence of Roosevelt's book is an overwhelming account of the natural history of Africa not easily available in one volume; but he also moves on to ethnology, lessons in game protection, and an astute record of the beginnings of European civilization in Eastern and Central Africa, "made more interesting by suggestive comparisons of that new country with regions of the United States, which thirty or forty years ago were almost as unsettled." [29] Grinnell had in mind, especially, Roosevelt's comparisons of the ranches of East Africa with those of the great plains of the American West.

So many enormous changes have taken place since *African Game Trails* was written that it is worth reading just to be startled by the world that was the British East Africa of seventy years ago. Many geographical names have changed; spellings have been altered; the hunters and whites are almost all gone; and the country has been divided into independent black nations. A modern reporter has written that one locates a lion today "by looking first for a circle of minibuses with tourists leaning out at all angles," [30] cameras in hand. Now big-game hunting is a depressed industry; "Tanzania has banned it altogether, and so has Uganda. In Kenya, only limited trophies are allowed." [31] Women naturalists live among gorillas and elephants whom they know by name. Color photography and telescopic lens have replaced the rifle. Roosevelt supplies a thorough record of a world that will never reappear as he saw it.

Roosevelt held the Aristotelian view that primitive races are inferior and that the march of civilization is ever upwards. Thus his views on the natives of Africa, although repudiated by current events, seem shocking when read today. Roosevelt believes emphatically that many sections of East Africa, for example, "can be made a white man's country; and in these parts every effort should be made to favor the growth of a large and prosperous white population." [32] He expected the whites to govern with wisdom and firmness in their own interests and in those of the black and brown races. These efforts would be accomplished by the united efforts of the officials and the missionaries. Lest anyone stigmatize Roosevelt for his racist views, it must be pointed out that Jack London had the same judgment of the superiority of the white race in 1900: "What the devil! I am first of all a white man, and only then a Socialist!" [33] The special calling of the white races to rule the world was commonly held

by most of Roosevelt's contemporaries.[34] His paternalism could
not envision the sons of his bearers one day comprising the
Mau Mau. Throughout the book he sees the natives as children
to be treated with firmness first and kindness second, and to be
tolerated in their innocent amusements. Roosevelt was not malicious in his views, nor was he inconsistent. He maintains this
attitude throughout the *African Game Trails*, having, no doubt,
his Romanes lecture to be delivered at Oxford at the end of his
safari in mind. The Romanes lecture was written before he left
Washington, for in the previous August he had been invited to
deliver one of the series of lectures given by naturalists since
1891. His views stated in the Romanes lecture are echoed in
African Game Trails. Although well-intentioned, the best that
can be said of his attitude is that it was meddling of the grossest
sort. He sought not to exploit, but to help—unfortunately, he
judged from a position of superiority. Today, the destiny of
Africa and the black and brown races is almost entirely in their
own hands.

It would not be fair to all of Roosevelt's book to dwell merely
on his outdated social and political views; actually his book is
a masterpiece of poetic observation of wildlife. *African Game
Trails* was not dictated to secretaries; it was written carefully,
chapter by chapter, by hand. In this book, as in *Through the
Brazilian Wilderness*, Roosevelt recovered the artistry of his earlier books. The "Foreword" begins as follows:

"I speak of Africa and golden joys"; the joy of wandering through
lonely lands; the joy of hunting the mighty and terrible lords of the
wilderness, the cunning, the wary, and the grim.

In these greatest of the world's great hunting-grounds there are
mountain peaks whose snows are dazzling under the equatorial sun;
swamps where the slime oozes and bubbles and festers in the steaming heat; lakes like seas; skies that burn above deserts where the iron
desolation is shrouded from view by the wavering mockery of the
mirage; vast grassy plains where palms and thorn-trees fringe the
dwindling streams; mighty rivers rushing out of the heart of the continent through the sadness of endless marshes; forests of gorgeous
beauty, where death broods in the dark and silent depths.

There are regions as healthy as the northland; and other regions,
radiant with bright-hued flowers, birds, and butterflies, odorous with
sweet and heavy scents, but treacherous in their beauty, and sinister
to human life. On the land and in the water there are dread brutes

that feed on the flesh of man; and among the lower things that crawl and fly and sting and bite, he finds swarming foes far more evil and deadly than any beast or reptile; foes that kill his crops and his cattle, foes before which he himself perishes in his hundreds of thousands.[35]

Roosevelt concludes his foreword:

These things can be told. But there are no words that can tell the hidden spirit of the wilderness, that can reveal its mystery, its melancholy, and its charm. There is delight in the hardy life of the open, in long rides rifle in hand, in the thrill of the fight with dangerous game. Apart from this, yet mingled with it, is the strong attraction of the silent places, of the large tropic moons, and the splendor of the new stars; where the wanderer sees the awful glory of sunrise and sunset in the wide waste spaces of the earth, unworn of man, and changed only by the slow change of the ages through time everlasting.[36]

The *Bookman* of October 1910 carried a feature article which sampled reviews of *African Game Trails* from newspapers around the country. The article recognizes the bias that then greeted every new book by Roosevelt in saying, "It is not surprising to find that *African Game Trails* as a book is very much obscured by the personality of its author, and that we can turn to a review and learn whether the newspaper in which it appears is for or against 'My Policies.' " [37] The *Galaxy*, for example, would have the book suppressed and dearly wished that the self-advertising vandal would never again be elected to the presidency. The *Springfield Sunday Union* thought the book written with fitting modesty. The *Chicago Record-Herald* saw qualities that raised it to the first rank of outdoor literature. The *Philadelphia Public Ledger* considered it a remarkable literary achievement. The *New York Tribune* called it the book of the year. The *Chicago Tribune* mourned the absence of literary style. The *Rochester Post-Express* could not envision Roosevelt as a Christian idealist; he had more in common with Nimrod than with St. Paul or Tolstoy. The fragment of a review in an Iowa paper which assigned the book to a feminine reporter is the most entertaining of all, as she vicariously reports: "There is a delight in the hardy life of the open, in long rides, rifle in hand; in the thrill of the fight with dangerous game. Apart from this, yet mingled with it, is the strong attraction of the silent places, of the large tropic moons, and the splendour of new stars, where the wanderer

sees the awful glory of sunrise and sunset in the wide places
of the earth, unworn of man and changed only by the slow
change of the ages through time everlasting." [38] Her paraphrase
of Roosevelt's foreword makes one wonder if she read anything
more but, in any event, heightens the effect of his manly, robust
prose.

VI   Through the Brazilian Wilderness *(1914)*

When Roosevelt was planning his trip to Africa in 1908, he
wrote to Lodge that he felt no longer fit to do arduous exploring
work and had no intentions for further activity of such a nature.
Yet he wanted ever to remain a man of action. Five years later,
when several South American countries invited him to address
various learned bodies, he once again decided on an adventure
at the conclusion of his lecture tour. He would avoid the travelled
routes, take along Kermit and two naturalists, George K. Cherrie
and Leo E. Miller, and go up the Paraguay River and across the
Amazon through central South America, where no collectors had
ever worked. However, in Brazil he was asked by the Brazilian
government to head, with their own Colonel Candido Rondon,
a party that would enter an unexplored portion of western Matto
Grosso, "to attempt the descent of a river which flowed nobody
knew whither, but which the best-informed men believed would
prove to be a very big river, utterly unknown to geographers." [39]
Roosevelt eagerly accepted, even though he was fifty-five years
old, blind in one eye, and seriously overweight. Thus began one
of the most astonishing stories of adventure ever recorded. Other
South American explorers, Henry Walter Bates at twenty-six,
Alfred Russel Wallace at twenty-three, Charles Darwin at
twenty-two on the *Beagle*, never went so far from the trail as did
Roosevelt at fifty-five.[40] Today the river is visible on any map
of South America and is labeled the Theodore Roosevelt River,
so named by Colonel Rondon and the Brazilian government.

The story of the expedition is told in a narrative that describes
in detail every event from the planning to the end of the exploration. Roosevelt wrote notes each evening and from these completed the entire story in a series that appeared in *Scribner's*
from April through November of 1914. The book, also issued in
1914, has an added few chapters that describe the events after
reaching signs of civilization, the work of the field geographer

and the field zoologist, and the proper outfit to be acquired for difficult travelling. As always in his writing, Roosevelt punctuates his narrative with observations on the natural life around him; therefore, the book is both a story of exploration and a naturalist's notebook blended in such a way that the whole is greater than the parts.

Roosevelt prefaces his account of the exploration of the Dúvida, or River of Doubt, with a great amount of natural history pertaining to the past and present of South America. Because the continent has the most extensive and most varied avifauna of all the continents, he feels obliged to render constant and extensive attention to the bird life and to make comparisons with the birds of North America. As for the mammals, they had suffered some strange catastrophe in the past; and sabretooth tigers, huge lions, camellike pachyderms, mylodons the size of rhinoceros, horses of many kinds, all disappeared abruptly, leaving the continent with a paucity of mammalian species. Most of his discussions of mammals focus upon the jaguar.

Unfortunately, the party begins its exploration during the rainy season; the plague of accompanying insects is described in detail. Venomous fire-ants and ticks forever crawl on the explorers; maribundi wasps attack them. Vicious little sand flies, called pium flies, bite them and leave little black specks on the skin for weeks. Black ants and mosquitoes assail them. At one point a column of carnivorous foraging ants comes straight through the camp between the kitchen and the sleeping tents. All of these difficulties, plus the dangers from the piranha fish, they face even before they reach the River of Doubt to begin their exploration.

On February 27, 1914, the party starts down the river into the unknown. They begin with the most unlikely kind of canoes— seven heavy dugouts. As they progress, they soon find serious obstacles in the form of impossible rapids. Thus begins the backbreaking work of hauling—and losing—heavy dugouts along the rapids. It is not unusual for the river to narrow from a hundred yards to two yards. Termites destroy mosquito-nets, ponchos, and duffel bags. Everyone is bitten and stung by bees, mosquitoes, and flies. Day after day the rapids impede the passage of the dugouts. Finally, when they begin to lose dugouts and supplies, the situation becomes grave. A first man is lost by drowning. Each difficult day is followed by one more difficult. Sickness and

injury begin to take their toll. By March 19 the party must build
more dugout canoes for survival. In three weeks they have gone
only eighty-seven miles and have no idea how far yet they would
travel. Some days they are fortunate to paddle for two hours
before coming to a series of impassable rapids requiring the
rolling of the canoes again on logs alongside the river wherever
they can make a clearing. Only the heroic efforts of Kermit,
Lieutenant Lyra, and Cherrie keep the group moving. "Their
clothes were never dry. Their shoes were rotten. The bruises
on their feet and legs had become sores. On their bodies some of
the insect bites had become festering wounds. . . ." [41] All of the
party was suffering horribly.

Suddenly a man is murdered by a renegade in the party. The
drama now heightens as Roosevelt relates the confusion of the
expedition. Dysentery and malaria begin to harass them further.
When the whole situation looks darkest, on April 15, the party
sees signs of civilized life along the river. They emerge, finally,
in triumph. The party put on the map a river of something over
nine hundred miles, the chief affluent of the Madeira, which is
itself the chief affluent of the Amazon. The naturalists have in
their trek collected 2,500 bird specimens and 500 mammals.

What Roosevelt did not tell was later revealed by Cherrie
and Kermit.[42] At one point Colonel Rondon saw the situation as
so hopeless that each man was to find his own way out if he
could. Roosevelt rejected this suggestion and kept the party together. When his own abscessed legs and malaria became so
bad that he could hardly walk, he urged Kermit and Cherrie
to continue without him. Roosevelt and the party, of course,
did come out of the jungle, but the trip eventually brought
Roosevelt an early death. In the book, Roosevelt does not mention even once his own pain or suffering as being enough to do
more than inconvenience him. His joy of life never left him.
John Evans, in his review of the book for the *Geographical
Journal* of February 15, 1915, expresses the true value of *Through
the Brazilian Wilderness*: "The great charm of this book is that
it is instinct with the personality of the author. Everywhere the
reader has before him the man himself and his indomitable
cheerfulness and courage; but the predominant note is his active
interest in the myriad forms of plant or animal existence that
are encountered, and there are few routes which could yield a

greater wealth of material for the open-air student of life in all its varieties than that traversed by the 'Expedicão Scientifica Roosevelt-Rondon.' " [43]

The stamp of Roosevelt's personality gives *Through the Brazilian Wilderness* its distinctive style: a constant tone of optimism, certainty in factual information, earnest good humor, sufficient self-effacement, and great storytelling. When Roosevelt, early in the book, speaks about snakes, he resorts to a fascinating story of a visit to an institute designed for the study of poisonous Brazilian snakes. The observations Roosevelt renders are a combination of boyish delight with the more outlandish aspects of man's experience with snakes, and the grave, careful scientific noting of facts by a field naturalist. He describes the vicious and truculent colubrine snake, tells how it strikes violently at him three times, and states that it is totally harmless. "One of the innumerable mysteries of nature which are at present absolutely insoluble is why some snakes should be so vicious and others absolutely placid and good-tempered." [44] In speaking of the mussurama snake, which he considers perhaps the most interesting snake in the world, he follows his habit of relating it to what he knows, in this instance the king snake of the United States, which has the same trait of feeding on other snakes yet is harmless to man. His personal responses evoke in the reader a toleration for a delicate topic that normally might provoke distaste or discomfort. Roosevelt handles the topic of snakes as nicely as he does the subject of birds.

Roosevelt always oriented himself to new surroundings through his intensive knowledge of birds. In South America he found hundreds of birds whose songs he did not know. Gradually he developed his understanding and recognition of the new bird-calls and songs by focusing on those already familiar to him or nearly so. His tender, appreciative listening can be seen in his response to a "shy" woodland thrush which lives near the ground but sings high among the branches: "At a great distance we could hear the ringing, musical, bell-like note, long drawn and of piercing sweetness, which occurs at intervals in the song; at first I thought this was the song, but when it was possible to approach the singer I found that these far-sounding notes were scattered through a continuous song of great melody." [45] Although he recounts instance after instance of successfully locating birds he longed to hear, he never claimed to hear all of them; he acknowledges that he "never heard the wonderful white-banded mocking-bird, which is said by Hudson, who knew well the birds of South American and Europe, to be the song-king of them all." [46] He admits that Cherrie and Miller, the naturalists, saw "many, many more" birds than he did. Nevertheless, this book is a book of bird life as much as a tale of exploration.

Roosevelt fascinates the reader also with his opinions on a great variety of topics, from the Catholic Church in South America to the growth of militarism. He beats the drum heavily for worldwide conservation of wildlife and urges the training of naturalists and historians who can write well.

This book surpasses all of his other outdoor books in comprehension, opinion, and observation. It is, plainly enough, a tale of extremely difficult exploration; but it also summarizes and caps the entire outdoor writing of Theodore Roosevelt. He may challenge his reader or even irritate him, but he will hold the reader's attention; he can never be dull. His childlike imagination, his gifted powers of observation, his willingness to learn, and his powerful vocabulary make this book one of his greatest achievements. His skill in dramatic interpretation can speak of trees murdering trees:

In one grove the fig-trees were killing the palms, just as in Africa they kill the sandalwood-trees. In the gloom of this grove there were no flowers, no bushes; the air was heavy; the ground was brown with mouldering leaves. Almost every palm was serving as a prop for a fig-tree. The fig-trees were in every stage of growth. The youngest ones merely ran up the palms as vines. In the next stage the vine had thickened and was sending out shoots, wrapping the palm stem in a deadly hold. Some of the shoots were thrown round the stem like the tentacles of an immense cuttlefish. Others looked like claws, that were hooked into every crevice, and round every projection. In the stage beyond this the palm had been killed, and its dead carcass appeared between the big, winding vine trunks; and later the palm had disappeared and the vines had united into a great fig-tree. Water stood in black pools at the foot of the murdered trees, and of the trees that had murdered them. There was something sinister and evil in the dark stillness of the grove; it seemed as if sentient beings had writhed themselves round and were strangling other sentient beings.[47]

No other book ever written conveys with more exactitude the fascinating horror of the South American jungle.

VII   A Book-Lover's Holidays in the Open *(1916)*

In 1916 Roosevelt wrote an enthusiastic appreciation of the
life of adventure outdoors as a foreword to *A Book-Lover's
Holidays in the Open*. He points out the strength and endurance
required for such a life and the great scenic portions of earth
available to anyone truly wanting to visit them. He concludes,
"The joy of living is his who has the heart to demand it." [48]

A Book-Lover's Holidays in the Open derives its title from
"Books for Holidays in the Open," which he wrote for the *Ladies'
Home Journal* of April 1915. The collection of magazine articles
first appeared in *Outlook* and *Scribner's*, except for the title
essay and two essays on the Navajo Desert and the Hopi Indians.
The contents of the book are only loosely related in some in-
stances, and not at all in others. The first three chapters deal
with the southwestern United States: "A Cougar-Hunt on the
Rim of the Grand Canyon," "Across the Navajo Desert," and
"The Hopi Snake-Dance." The next three are a supplement to
Through the Brazilian Wilderness. The remaining six essays
deal with a variety of outdoor topics.

Roosevelt develops an entirely new topic in this volume, the
experiences in the Navajo Desert with the Hopi Indians. As
usual, he is graphically effective in his descriptions of the desert
country. And, as always, he digresses to speak of the Indian
problem in general. He insists that Indian lawlessness has hurt
the whites out of proportion to anything done to the Indians,
a position he had held since writing *The Winning of the West*.
He regrets that cultural advances by certain tribes were destroyed constantly by more savage tribes. As a past president,
Roosevelt was privileged to be taken not only to the Indian
dances, but to a secret snake-ceremony in a kiva as well. He
shows true discernment and courtesy in appreciation of the
privilege and has left a valuable, authentic eye-witness report
of these practices.

The book supplements *Through the Brazilian Wilderness*, for
he tells of his visits to Argentina and Chile, as well as Brazil.
Each essay dwells upon the colorful and adventuresome. Roosevelt also gives further recollections and impressions of his African
trip, many of them purposefully taking issue with his adversaries,
the "philanthropists," a term today which would be "do-gooders."
He also manages to support other favorite themes, such as the
necessity of large, healthy families for the welfare of the nation.

Roosevelt devotes a considerable amount of space to "Primeval Man." In this essay he considers man's earliest years on earth, and dazzles the reader with his breadth of knowledge and his theories. In one instance, he wonders about the failure of the American Indian to tame animals. He observes that they stayed on a level of civilization similar to that of the African tribes. The Indians failed to tame the American species of buffalo or other animals just as the Africans never tamed their buffalo or eland, and both peoples had to await the arrival of animals tamed elsewhere.

Roosevelt's theories even range back over the Pleistocene and Eocene epochs, with a tremendous sense of excitement as he describes the development and disappearance of species in his ruminations. He calls to mind the Greeks and the Carthaginians, the Dutch and the Arabs in his visions of the past. His purpose is joy, "just for joy's sake." [49] The fascination with the past was a living experience for him, and he advises that it should be so for all travelers and politicians. After a symphony of history and animals in history, he ends on a tranquil note: "Of all the wonderful great beasts with which primitive man in his most primitive forms has been associated, the three with which on the whole this association was most wide-spread in time and space were the horse, the lion, and the elephant." [50] Roosevelt's knowledge of the grand sweep of history and his enthusiasm, to paraphrase him, must strongly appeal to every person interested in the teeming life of the past; each would want to feel the keen delight known to those who care intensely for the life of thought and the life of action.

The title essay, "Books for Holidays in the Open," is the kind of survey that still appears regularly in the American press when book supplements or reviewers suggest summer reading. Roosevelt says the books for outdoors are no different from those read at home. He then proceeds to name some of his favorites— those which were in the Pigskin Library of books he carried in Africa. Many authors he would read over and over, such as Gibbon, Macaulay, some of Shakespeare, and much of Dickens. He believed a person could judge his own moral tone by the nature of the books that attracted him.

He also gives a revealing explanation of his interest in a particular subject. He would begin with a current book, become interested in comments or references in the book, and then move on to check those, and then on to others: "My study of and delight in Mahan sent me farther afield, to read queer old volumes about De Ruyter and the daring warrior-merchants of Hansa, and to study, as well as I could, the feats of Suffren and Tegethoff. I did not need to study Farragut." [51] Such an essay is designed to provoke excitement and love of reading; no doubt the veneration Roosevelt had for books from his earliest days to his last moments will impress anyone who reads it today.

VIII *Papers on Natural History*

Throughout his writing career, Roosevelt published articles on natural history, many of them arising from controversies, such as the dispute about "Protective Coloration." Concealing coloration, as related to the survival of species, Roosevelt readily acknowledged; but he could not subscribe to a universal application of the principle as did Abbott H. Thayer and Gerald H. Thayer in *Concealing Coloration in the Animal Kingdom.* Roosevelt reinforced his own arguments on the subject while in Africa, to form an appendix for *African Game Trails.* Other articles on the topic appeared in the *American Museum Journal,* the *Journal of Experimental Zoology,* and elsewhere. The debate caught the attention of naturalists all over the United States. Roosevelt is hardly reticent in stating his case with the usual certainty that he acquired in debate during his Harvard days. Sure of his facts, and supported by convincing illustrations, he exhausts his opponents, even if he does not defeat them in every instance.

Another argument that lingered and produced extensive debate was the matter of "nature-faking." [52] Roosevelt resented the fictionalizing of animal behavior for palatable consumption by school children. His cry of "Realism is truth" persisted throughout the weeks of controversy. Roosevelt respected the work of animal writers such as Stewart Edward White, but he saw only harm in the false teaching of animal behavior in the stories of Jack London or, even worse, William J. Long. Thompson Seton and Charles D. G. Roberts also came under his attack. Roosevelt's articles "Animal Coloration," "Protective Coloration," and "Men Who Misinterpret Nature" still make instructive reading. But "Nature Fakers," if taken too literally, would bankrupt the Disney enterprises. Roosevelt will not tolerate playfulness, even in the cause of entertainment for children, if the authors take any liberty whatsoever with the facts of natural history.

One of his last nature essays, titled "My Life as a Naturalist" and published in the *American Museum Journal* of May 1918, sums up his career better than anything anyone else could say of him as a naturalist. In the first sentence he makes no pretentions, calling himself an amateur naturalist. He confesses that he never had an interest in invertebrates. He acknowledges that his idols were of a past generation, men like John James Audubon and Charles Waterton, and that he "sat at the feet" of Charles Darwin and Thomas Henry Huxley. In the most modest terms he traces his career in the study of nature, deprecating most of his early work. He admits his disenchantment with formal study at Harvard because of the adoption of overprecise German methodology and the trend away from "naturalist," as "old-fashioned," to the adoption of "biologist" to indicate the new techniques. [53] Making no pretense of grand contributions, he modestly suggests that the books that traced life-histories of the large game of North America—*Hunting Trips of a Ranchman, Ranch Life and the Hunting Trail,* and *The Wilderness Hunter*—were of value, and "gave a good deal of information, which as far as I know, is not to be found elsewhere." [54] He considers his work on the cougar as outlined in *Outdoor Pastimes of an American Hunter* of "real value." *Through the Brazilian Wilderness* he calls primarily a work of exploration. His chief contributions to science, he feels, are to be found in *African Game Trails* and the book following it, *Life Histories of African Game Animals*, which he wrote in collaboration with Edmund Heller.

He concludes "My Life as a Naturalist":

I do not think there is much else for me to say about my anything but important work as a naturalist. But perhaps I may say further that while my interest in natural history has added very little to my sum of achievement, it has added immeasurably to my sum of enjoyment in life. [55]

The fact that he did enjoy his life outdoors so very much transmits itself on every page of his books of outdoor life. The zest for living, the love of new sights and sounds, the thrill of discovery, the awe of nature's landscapes, genuine appreciation of companionship, and the refusal to quit mark all of his books of outdoor life. They will always stand as reliable evidence for a world that has passed away. His constant appeals for conservation put him among the first in the United States who made possible the saving of the little that has been saved for future generations.

CHAPTER 4

Journalist

THROUGHOUT his political career and during the intervals while he was out of public office, Theodore Roosevelt wrote steadily for publication in newspapers and magazines. When he left the White House, he became a full-time journalist, at first for *Outlook* and later for *Metropolitan* and *The Kansas City Star*; he also continued to write articles, introductions, and addresses which were published elsewhere.

In writing of the ancient Greek leader Solon, whose career corresponded in so many respects with Roosevelt's, Gerald F. Else points out that after Solon completed his work of arbitration and settlement, he "laid down his office and went abroad on prolonged travels." [1] Else continues:

He was not only the greatest statesman of archaic Athens, he was her greatest and only literary man. A certain amount of ink has been spilled, to little purpose, over the question whether Solon was a great poet. Whether he was or not, he was a born writer, a man who felt an insistent need to communicate his thoughts and feelings to more men than happened to be within range of his voice at the moment, and beyond the immediate issues of the moment. Moreover, although he treasured the "good things" of life all his days—love, friendship, wine, horses, and dogs—most of his writing centered on public questions. Nowadays much of it would be called—ugly word!—"journalistic." In any case its predominant aim was persuasion and, in a higher sense, instruction. [2]

Roosevelt was searching, always, for the same unity and freedom for his people that Solon sought, and Roosevelt knew as well that it had to be a moral and spiritual unity. The simple virtues that Roosevelt sought were the same "Courage, tenacity, faithfulness, courtesy and consideration, above all the dedication of one's whole being, up to and including life itself, to an overriding ideal of nobility" [3] that Solon looked for in the Greek people. William Allen White, in an introduction to Roosevelt's *American Ideals*, sumarizes as well as anyone the Old Testament flavor of Roosevelt's style in his exhortations: "No tall talk about schemes of redemption nor plans of atonement and no soft amenities of a free grace and undying love are found in these simple exhortations." [4]

I Literary Essays *(1926)*

The most distinguished of Roosevelt's essays, derived largely from his magazine articles, have been collected into volume twelve of his *Works*, under the title *Literary Essays*. (An earlier version of his best essays consisted of the first nine in this volume and was published with the title *History as Literature* by Scribner's in 1913.) The expanded version of fifty essays reflects the thoughts of a man interested in all facets of modern life. The essays are opinionated, assertive, controversial, and delightful. They are, in effect, the reader's listening to Roosevelt hold forth on an immense variety of topics that stimulated the people of his time. The essays demonstrate, first of all, Roosevelt's concentration of study in the field of history, but they also reveal him as perhaps the outstanding generalist of his era. Besides history, his essays touch upon foreign literatures, art, natural history, geography, race, the problems of minorities, and politics.

The first nine essays in this collection deserve special attention, since Roosevelt himself first chose them for separate publication. The title essay, "History as Literature," focuses upon the need for history to be taken as a science and turned into literature. Roosevelt's indebtedness to James Harvey Robinson, historian and one of the founders of the New School for Social Research, he amply indicates. He believes, furthermore, that some historians, through art and genius, can make their subjects great, and concludes by forecasting the future of the nation as it moves to industrialism and a new ethnic type.

His next essay, "Biological Analogies in History," is likely read today by more college students than anything else by Roosevelt. It appears in a college anthology of works inspired by the evolutionist Charles Darwin.[5] The essay was delivered to the students of Oxford University in Oxford, England, in 1910. Although it has some muddy explanations of race and "stock," the essay contains noteworthy comparisons between species of the animal world and species of societies, the disappearance of either being a challenging mystery. A common purpose held by all the people in a nation, Roosevelt says, unaffected of blood but knit by a bond of speech and culture, will insure survival. Sometimes this unity must be preserved even, as in the case of the United States, by a civil war. The point of national character, as in the exalted case of the Romans, is to leave a mark on the history of mankind.

Also while in Europe in 1910, Roosevelt spoke to the students at the University of Berlin. The title of the essay based on that speech itself carries an exciting prospect for those interested in the rise and fall of civilizations and the general direction of world history. In "The World Movement" he says much that was never expanded until Marshall McLuhan and other futurists in our own time recognized and elaborated the effect of technology on human life in the Global Village. Roosevelt provokes comparison in saying, "Islam arose, and conquered far and wide, uniting fundamentally different races into a brotherhood of feeling which Christianity has never been able to rival, and at the time of the Crusades profoundly influencing European culture." [6] He believes the invention of printing and the discovery of America to have changed civilization, "not only in degree but even in kind from all that that had gone before." [7] Later he adds, "Now steam and electricity have worked a complete revolution; and the resulting ease of communication has in its turn changed all the physical questions of human life." [8] Twice he mentions the coming conquest of the air. The essay is both challenging and visionary.

In "Productive Scholarship" Roosevelt pays tribute to the "production by scholarly men which is not, strictly speaking, scholarship." [9] And he revives his oft-stated argument that "professional scholars sometimes actually distrust scholarship which is able . . . to bring forth wisdom divorced from pedantry and dryness." [10] The remainder of the essay is a review of four books which evinces Roosevelt's generosity as a critic. He chose usually to review books of authors whom he admired—in this essay they are *The Medieval Mind* by Henry Osborn Taylor, *The Life and Times of Cavour* by William Roscoe Thayer, and *The Early Literary Career of Browning* and *The Yale Book of American Verse*, both by Thomas R. Lounsbury. The first two books are commented upon in very general terms of appreciation; Browning, however, receives considerable attention from Roosevelt, who had a lifelong strongly ambivalent relationship with Browning's poems. Browning's more obscure poems have always inspired the laughter that stays tears, and Roosevelt appreciates the frustration in quoting Lounsbury: "In fact, commentaries on Browning generally bear a close resemblance to foghorns. They proclaim the existence of a fog, but they do not disperse it." [11] The last book does not especially please Roosevelt because of the improbability of ever choosing an anthology that could please everyone.

"Dante and the Bowery" may seem an unlikely topic for an essay. Roosevelt, who reread and discussed Dante's work at every opportunity, realized that the Bowery in New York represents a kind of hell. He expands his analogy to compare the war of the Ghibellines and Guelphs with the American Civil War and the characters in them. Then Jesse James and Billy the Kid come to mind as candidates for judgment, and a host of others. Roosevelt suggests that we have lost the ability to express ourselves in epics, and with it a simplicity of soul that can see the good and evil around us as related to that of the past. Roosevelt does in this essay what he does in his historical essays: he chooses to make correspondences between the present and the past, and he is arrestingly effective in so doing. The breadth of his comparisons shows a love for Dante's poem and a deep respect for Dante's moral courage.

It is simple today to see the implicit dangers in *The Foundations of the Nineteenth Century*, by Houston Stewart Chamberlain. This book, reviewed by Roosevelt in an essay with the same title for *Outlook*, stands as a racist document of Teutonic pretensions of the kind that led straight to Adolph Hitler's ravings. Although Roosevelt held strong opinions on race, he was not gulled by this anti-Semitic tract. He sees some merit in certain features of Chamberlain's book, such as its appreciation of Christianity and the sketches of early Roman history; however, he recognizes what he calls Chamberlain's intellectual antics. At one point in his essay he remarks, "Mr. Chamberlain himself is quite as fantastic an extremist as any of those he derides, and an extremist whose doctrines are based on foolish hatred is even more unlovely than an extremist whose doctrines are based on foolish benevolence." [12] More than once Roosevelt questions

Chamberlain's sanity. Those who find Roosevelt's attitudes on race questionable at best would do well to read this essay, in which he drew the line beyond which he would not go. He does not dismiss the book in righteous passion; he calmly dissects the thesis and discards what is trash. Prophetically, the last words of his essay calls the idea "an influence to be reckoned with and seriously to be taken into account." [13]

In "The Search for Truth in a Reverent Spirit" Roosevelt begins, "There is superstition in science quite as much as there is superstition in theology, and it is all the more dangerous because those suffering from it are profoundly convinced that they are freeing themselves from all superstition." [14] His purpose in this essay is to examine the theses of a number of books that touch upon religion and evolution, including works by Henri Bergson, Carlos Reyles, Henry Osborn Taylor, Émile Boutroux, and at least six others. For Roosevelt this essay must be classified as his finest intellectual pyrotechnical display. Ideas flash out of every sentence as he pursues the search for truth, renouncing the absolutism of the materialists, repudiating the retreat to reactionary medievalism, and imploring fundamental agreement by all truth-seekers. Roosevelt was too educated a man to be taken in by mere reason: "True wisdom must necessarily refuse to allow reason to assume a sway outside of its limitations; and where experience plainly proves that the intellect has reasoned wrongly, then it is the part of wisdom to accept the teachings of experience, and bid reason be humble—just as under like conditions it would bid theology be humble." [15] And later he writes, "So in the world of the intellect it is easy to take the position of the hard materialists who rail against religion, and easy also to take the position of those whose zeal for orthodoxy makes them distrust all action by men of independent mind in the search for scientific truth; but it is not so easy to make it understood that we both acknowledge our inestimable debt to the great masters of science, and yet are keenly alive to their errors and decline to surrender our judgment to theirs when they go wrong." [16] Roosevelt concludes sensibly, "We must stand equally against tyranny and against irreverence in all things of the spirit, with the firm conviction that we can all work together for a higher social and individual life if only, whatever form of creed we profess, we make the doing of duty and the love of our fellow men two of the prime articles in our universal faith." [17]

Roosevelt was something of an authority on "The Ancient Irish Sagas," and certainly was a highly informed and devoted reader of ancient Celtic literature, as he proves in the essay of that title. In his time little was known of the Celtic sagas in America. Roosevelt tells of the imprecise origin of the sagas, their grouping in cycles—Cuchulain, Ossianic—and their value for historians. His appreciation of this literature is not feigned; he summarizes the stories in considerable detail and does so affectionately. He finds it charming that the women in these sagas are so individual and so human, such as Emer and Deirdre. Actually, he considers these women quite modern in their attitudes and behavior. Roosevelt's purpose is to make the sagas more widely appreciated and to share one of his own great delights.

The final essay of the original group first published together is "An Art Exhibition." Anyone who has visited Roosevelt's home at Oyster Bay, New York, can imagine his response upon entering the International Exhibition of Modern Art at New York in 1913. Roosevelt's tastes did not run toward the very modern, although some of the paintings in his home are in the style of Joseph Mallord Turner. Roosevelt offers one priceless opinion at the start of his essay of bafflement: "It is true, as the champions of these extremists say, that there can be no life without change, no development without change, and that to be afraid of what is different or unfamiliar is to be afraid of life. It is no less true, however, that change may mean death and not life, and retrogression instead of development." [18]

What this essay does more than to criticize the radical direction that painting and sculpture was taking is to reveal how Roosevelt's mind worked when it was confronted with what it could not really understand. There is the mild declamation, of course, and the controlled contempt; yet there is the latent willingness to understand and a final generous appreciation for as much as he can appreciate. Unless something were patently immoral, Roosevelt would not dismiss it out of hand, although in this essay he occasionally comes close. The man who knew everything is dramatically forced to realize that the world was moving ahead too quickly for him. Roosevelt did bring America into the modern age, but it left him in the past. Few men in history have stood so symbolically at a watershed of time as Roosevelt did at the International Exhibition of Modern Art.

The remaining forty-one essays are in the general areas of the first nine, except that the last fifteen touch upon topics of natural history, hunting, conservation, and exploration. Roosevelt takes many positions in his essays that are highly controversial. Because he thought large families essential to the survival of the nation, he takes every opportunity to chastise men and women who refuse to have more than one or two children. (He privately involved himself in a debate by correspondence with George Bernard Shaw on this topic. [19]) He considered the matter neither jocular nor unimportant, and he singles out the New England conscience for tolerating concepts of "race suicide." Yet, in his emphasis on survival of the race he adds purity as well, even to the extent that he would sterilize criminals and prohibit the feeble-minded from leaving children behind them. Others may think materialism has subverted America beyond redemption, but Roosevelt continued to look for a moral awakening in men and women to their sense of responsibility. Throughout his *Literary Essays* he writes of the need for homely, everyday, all-important virtues and of the vice of morbid and false sentimentality. He continues his controversial assertions by depicting Tolstoy as a threat to morality, and the legislative decisions of the Supreme Court as undemocratic as government by a hereditary aristocracy.

All of these essays are written with Roosevelt's customary declarative style. Often he will lapse into an awkwardness of structure that cannot conceal the rapidity with which he composed. For Roosevelt, what is to be said is far more important than how it is to be said. The intensity of his opinions directed his art. The breadth of his informed opinions was rivaled only by the depth of his knowledge in so many fields of human thought. His gift of total recall served him well in his profession as an essayist. None of these essays has the mark of superficiality. Roosevelt did his homework, and he knew what he wanted to say. For those who understand Roosevelt's nature, his opinions and assertions are not hazards to appreciating him. He loved argument for its own sake; he would not give an inch in disputation. To those who attribute malicious intention to Roosevelt, these essays may seem abrasive; to those who see him as searching honestly for the truth, and demanding nothing less than the truth in all subjects, they reveal not only much information but also Roosevelt himself.

II American Ideals *(1897)*

In February 1905 Barrett Wendell, first professor of American literature at Harvard, was in France and wrote at the request of M. Peixotte an article on Theodore Roosevelt for the French review *Revue Politique et Parlementaire.* Wendell wrote to Henry Cabot Lodge and enclosed a copy of the article, in English, for Lodge to show to the President if it seemed appropriate. In the article Wendell traces the character and development of Roosevelt and explains Roosevelt's appeal to all classes of men, but most of all stresses Roosevelt's breaking the barrier against men of his class participating in politics.[20]

The principal theme of Roosevelt's *American Ideals* concentrates precisely on Wendell's point that men of education and wealth should be active in political life on all levels of government and that men must possess the manly virtues of personal courage, physical and moral, to do good work in politics. Criticizing is not enough. Politics is too important to be left to the manipulators of the immigrant masses who will let the critics have the virtue if they can have the efficiency. Roosevelt believed wholeheartedly in the need of moral courage in politics because "The voice of the people is not always the voice of God; and when it happens to be the voice of the devil, then it is a man's clear duty to defy its behests." [21]

Roosevelt in these essays appeals for an America culturally independent of Europe. He wants immigrants to leave their languages and customs behind them and pities the immigrant who cannot when he states, "If he tries to retain his old language, in a few generations it becomes a barbarous jargon; if he tries to retain his old customs and ways of life, in a few generations he becomes an uncouth boor." [22] Everyone must throw himself heart and soul into the work of America. Roosevelt decries the colonialism of Canada in his time and wants no such subservience to England by the United States either directly or indirectly.

As for the masses of the people, he wants them to recognize the necessity in the American system for wealth in the community which really benefits all. His view is, "The worst foe of the poor man is the labor leader, whether philanthropist or politician, who tries to teach him that he is a victim of conspiracy and injustice, when in reality he is merely working out his fate with

blood and sweat as the immense majority of men who are worthy
of the name have always done and always will have to do." [23]
No quack remedies of social engineering appealed to Roosevelt,
legislative or otherwise. An American must rely on himself, in
Roosevelt's view, and not on the State. If inordinate circumstances developed, then law should support any individual or
group of individuals oppressed.

Returning in *American Ideals* to his topic of concern for any
decline in the population, he declares that in this world only a
strong nation can survive. He wants one great nation and not
a "contemptible knot of struggling nationalities." [24] The China
of his time, a mere aggregate of provinces, serves as his example
of weakness, and he accurately predicts, "China will not menace
Siberia until after undergoing some stupendous and undreamed-
of internal revolution." [25] Earnestly committed to the idea of a
strong America, he states, "Diplomacy is utterly useless where
there is no force behind it; the diplomat is the servant, not the
master, of the soldier." [26] Understanding very well the process
of change and giving the lie to those who saw him as a flag-
waving patriot, he places all in proportion when he says, "Patriotism, love of country, and pride in the flag which symbolizes
country may be feelings which the race will at some period
outgrow, but at present they are very real and strong, and the
man who lacks them is a useless creature, a mere incumbrance
to the land." [27]

George Merriam Hyde in the *Bookman* of January 1898 said
the worst that can be said of Roosevelt's *American Ideals,* that
Roosevelt sees only black and whites. Hyde offered this judgment of the volume: "Pugnacity and an undefined, and un-
definable intense and fervid Americanism are his two dominant
ideas, which he applies at random to every human situation
and reiterates, in the manner of Cato rather than St. John, on
every page." [28] Hyde evidently did not allow for the youthful
idealism of the Roosevelt who produced almost every one of
these essays before he was thirty-five years of age, and who
had already felt the contumely of political attack and had determined to stay on the offensive. In his preface to the volume
Roosevelt states quite clearly that he is writing to move men
to action. He appropriately borrows a metaphor from the football
field to stir men from their drawing rooms to the arena—"that
there must be no shirking, and that success can come only to

the player who 'hits the line hard.' " [29] Throughout the book
Roosevelt invokes the style of the football coach urging his players into aggressive play. Whimpering withdrawal and resigned
pessimism would never raise the standards of public life in
Roosevelt's game. In these essays he preaches the doctrine of
practical, hard work from the ward to the presidency.

III   The Strenuous Life *(1900)*

Roosevelt never denied that he considered himself a lay
preacher who chose to preach realizable ideals, or that he considered the presidency the best pulpit in the world. When asked
by one of the students at Cambridge, England, to refrain from
preaching at them, Roosevelt replied, "I will promise to preach
as little as I can, but you must take your chance, for it is impossible to break the habit of a lifetime at the bidding of a comparative stranger." [30] And preach at them he did, on the conditions of success—not great success which comes by chance, but
the success of leading a decent life so that those dependent on
a man and attached to him are better for his having lived. Further, he told the students that no president enjoyed himself more,
nor any ex-president.

Roosevelt's lay sermons in *The Strenuous Life* were first published in book form by the Century Company in 1900 and considerably enlarged in subsequent editions. Its appearance as the
thirteenth volume of the *Works* is a reprint of the large third
edition; it consists of thirty-three essays. The central themes
are the importance of the homely virtues, the necessity of helping oneself, and the requirement that one throw himself
wholeheartedly into the task at hand. To Roosevelt, this same
aggressive morality applies as well to nations as to individuals.
A strong nation has the obligation to spread order and civilization; no other course can bring peace to this world. What one
nation refuses to do, another will do. He deplores the "unhealthy
peace-mysticism" of Tolstoy. Rather, it behooves both nations
and individuals to function with gusto to do what must be done.
He insists that the cultivation of moral strength is the first pre-
requisite of real success. Throughout the essays he uses historical
references and biographical allusions to make his point. Ulysses
S. Grant becomes useful as an example of unshakable strength
and perservering courage; Admiral Dewey stands for prepared-

ness and the acceptance of responsibility. More than anything, Roosevelt wants each person to stand on his own two feet and to ignore the call of the sentimentalist, whose largeness of heart invariably degenerates to softness of the head. True, he states, the industrial development of the nineteenth century produced great dangers as well as great benefits; yet thrift, energy, and self-mastery will insure success. "The wilfully idle man, like the wilfully barren woman, has no place in a sane, healthy, and vigorous community." [31]

He steadily alternates between the duties of the country and the duties of the individual. Harkening back to the Spanish-American War, he reminds his audience of the risks that must be taken from time to time in order to do good. He claims that the United States acted with disinterestedness in rescuing the Cubans from Spanish oppression, and spent huge sums in bringing education, sanitation, law and order, and prosperity to Cuba. He ends: "And now we are establishing them in a free and independent commonwealth, and have asked in return nothing whatever save that at no time shall their independence be prostituted to the advantage of some foreign rival of ours, or so as to menace our well-being. To have failed to ask this would have amounted to national stultification on our part." [32] (On his visit to the Sorbonne in 1910 Roosevelt preached the same themes in English and French to the students assembled there. He stressed the importance of lofty ideals, warned against cynicism, asked for the cultivation of "commonplace everyday qualities and virtues," and in fear of France's declining birth rate asked for the producing of more children. Roosevelt warned against the persuasion of doctrinaire speculation, recommending instead individual initiative. Socialism he saw as a threat to social justice.)

The Strenuous Life has a strict consistency; if a man or a nation is going to be ready at all times to act, then the results of the action will depend in large measure on prior disposition—in other words, on character. At no point does one reach a plateau or point of neutrality. Everyone is asked to be more. Life has no place of ease, only effort. Roosevelt's words to the boys of the preparatory school at Groton pertain to the people of any fine institution: "You are not entitled, either in college or in after-life, to an ounce of privilege because you have been at Groton—not an ounce; but we are entitled to hold you to an exceptional accountability because you have been at Groton." [33]

At the head of *The Strenuous Life* Roosevelt placed lines from Tennyson's "Ulysses." The transformation of Ulysses from the defeated figure in Dante's *Inferno* to a romantic idealist corresponds to Roosevelt's own romantic idealization of individual and national behavior. The usual affairs of nations and persons rarely ever reach the level of disinterestedness that Roosevelt seeks. All in all, his vision was romantic and for that reason likely to be revived from time to time as a relief from the tawdry life of self-seeking. Roosevelt offered an ideal not that men live by, but an ideal whereby they ought to live.

IV   *Political Writings*

Four volumes of Roosevelt's *Works* are collections of his political writings and addresses: *Campaigns and Controversies, State Papers as Governor and President, American Problems,* and *Social Justice and Popular Rule.* Admittedly these volumes may not appeal much to the general reader; but though they are of most interest to students of political history, many of the essays also offer Roosevelt's best thoughts on a variety of topics, including law, reform, progressivism, race relations, conservation, and the regulation of corporations.

Campaigns and Controversies (1926)

Campaigns and Controversies, a collection comprising Volume XIV of the *Works,* contains political writings and addresses which Roosevelt produced from the time of his entry into political life until he became president. When one considers the many important offices which he held, no doubt exists on the importance of his writings in reflecting the political climate of his time. From the first days of his career he stressed the importance of honesty and courage and even private morality in public life. When just a young man, he heard in Buffalo a Reverend Mr. Slicer phrase a doctrine which Roosevelt took to heart and adopted as his own—what was needed in political life was "not genius nor brilliancy, so much as the ordinary humdrum qualities and virtues, common sense, courage, integrity." [34] This simple commitment to decency marked all of his political expres-

sion and all his activities. Sometimes his simple honesty led to
unpopular positions with the public as in his decision while New
York Police Commissioner to close the beer halls on Sundays.
He constantly offered the adoption of the simple virtues as the
solution to the most complicated and vexing social problems. For
example, he was sensitive to the plight of the Negro in America,
yet he had a demanding attitude of hard work in any solution to
their problems. He saw privilege as a threat to America and came
down especially hard on "anglomaniacs." "Be Americans pure
and simple!" [35] Being Americans meant to venerate the homely
virtues. It is no wonder he opposed admitting Utah as a State
until the Mormon Church would change its attitude on polyg-
amy. His same simple solutions often were tinged with irony.
When a German anti-Semite came to the United States to speak
in New York, Roosevelt granted him freedom of speech and
undid much of Dr. H. Ahlwardt's mischief with the ridicule of
having Jewish policemen selected as his bodyguards.

Many of Roosevelt's positions would be unpopular today. He
felt it was infinitely better for the world that Russia had taken
Turkestan; France, Algiers; and England, India. He urged that
the United States carry the flag to every corner of the world in
the interests of civilization. He honestly believed that every
expansion of a civilized country was a conquest for peace and
that American expansionism would extend liberty and order. The
problem of exploitation escaped him. Roosevelt undoubtedly produced more "mugwumps" than had any other Republican before
him. His utterances lost him many friends. Ambrose Bierce and
a number of intellectuals expected him to one day be "Theodorus
Primus, Dei Gratia Rex et Imperator, Fidei Defensor"—Theodore
the first, by the grace of God, King and Emperor, Defender of
the Faith—with his seal bearing the polyglot motto "Ich Dien,—
Honni Soit Qui Mal y Pense!"—I serve,—Evil to him who thinks
evil.[36] Even earlier, Barrett Wendell thought Roosevelt capable
of seizing the government by force.[37]

State Papers as Governor and Presidential Addresses (1926)

State Papers as Governor and Presidential Addresses can be
recognized as Roosevelt's work first by their overt moral tone.
He was never subtle in dealing with the public: "It is absolutely
impossible for a republic long to endure if it becomes either

corrupt or cowardly; if its public men, no less than its private men, lose the indispensable virtue of honesty, if its leaders of thought become visionary doctrinaires, or if it shows a lack of courage in dealing with the many grave problems which it must surely face, both at home and abroad, as it strives to work out the destiny meet for a mighty nation." [38] Just as forthright in his dealing with the problem of predatory capitalism, he wanted to protect the individual against wrongs by the rich; but he did not oppose the growth of wealth derived by service to the community. In contemporary terms, he would give to the corporations and men of wealth the same opportunities to amass wealth as that given to the professional entertainer.

The various Presidential Annual Messages convey the compelling interests of the nation at the time of their delivery. Roosevelt forwarded eight Messages, and each contains over thirty items of national concern between 1901 and 1908. A considerable amount of information is compacted into these short sections, each with the stamp of Roosevelt's personality. Any student of American history will find them absorbing and characteristic of Roosevelt's political and moral thought.

American Problems (1926)

A representative sampling of Roosevelt's other addresses as President has been collected into *American Problems*, Volume XVI of the *Works*. (A more comprehensive collection can be found in the eight-volume Review of Reviews edition of *Presidential Addresses and State Papers* issued in 1910.)

The essays in *American Problems* touch upon all areas of interest to Roosevelt during his time in office. He shows his habits of calling attention to Civil War veterans in his audience, of appealing for the practice of homely virtues, of confronting the changes wrought by steam and electricity, of warning how the ascendency of one class to dominance will destroy a democracy, of asking women to be responsible mothers, and of constantly appealing for military preparedness. His precision in words and phrase-making make him always coherent. Enthusiasm for progress and civilization garnish all his efforts. Because he believed in the republican form of government and the fact that people must govern themselves, virtue in every man and woman became as important as government itself, and for this reason he

played the role of a lay preacher. In Roosevelt's work it is impossible to make any distinction between political speeches and
those dealing with good citizenship.

Social Justice and Popular Rule (1926)

Social Justice and Popular Rule contains political essays
written after Roosevelt left the White House. He had started a
movement of Progressivism while president, a movement which
he would not permit to be halted. His efforts he considered as
important as the work of the soldiers in the Civil War, to whom
he always alluded. His "square deal" would save the Union from
the onslaught of greedy wealth and would help the working man
ready to help himself.

Roosevelt's most brilliant writing in these essays deals with
the law and the Supreme Court. No higher compliment could be
given than that of Justice Benjamin N. Cardozo, who said of
Roosevelt that although he "was not a jurist, his intuitions
and perceptions were deep and brilliant." [39] Cardozo admits
his own regard for Roosevelt's Message of 1908. Roosevelt's full
relationship with the Supreme Court and the legal thought of
the United States has never been completely explored. He did
much to liberalize legal thinking and the judicial system. He put
Oliver Wendell Holmes on the Supreme Court, lauded and promoted Roscoe Pound's theories of sociological jurisprudence,
and was personal mentor to Federal Judge Learned Hand and
Justice Felix Frankfurter, both his dedicated political followers.

In his writings on constitutional law in this volume, Roosevelt
ponders the complexities of a conservative court halting economic and social progress. This same problem, to some journal-
ists, exists in our own time when a leading journal asks in a
banner cover headline, "Has the Supreme Court Abandoned the
Constitution?" [40] Roosevelt was squarely in the corner of those
who would extend human rights to include social and economic
rights. If the courts constantly invalidate legislative action by
another branch of the government, what recourse is left for the
relief of the people? It is an impossible question, particularly
since Roosevelt and many good men also believed that Justice
John Marshall, a Federalist who ignored many of the Jeffersonian ideas of democracy in favor of a strong judiciary, was
correct in doing so. Although Franklin Delano Roosevelt faced

the same problem but found no solution, Theodore Roosevelt
theorized over it in articles such as "The Recall of Judicial Decisions," and seriously considered the innovation of recalling
judges. For his daring exploration of this complex problem, he
has sometimes been called a "naive opportunist" or worse.[41] Yet,
the fact remains that the problem is still there. Roosevelt's solutions by recall of judges and the exercise of referendum by the
people in a certain class of decisions of constitutional questions
were alarming when he made them, and they still are; however,
he was willing to theorize over the problem, even though the passage of time seems to be the only remedy. Well aware of the
threat of the tyranny of the majority suggested by Alexis de
Tocqueville, Roosevelt feared worse that entrenched men of
privilege would forever frustrate social reform as long as the
judges sided with them in reactionary, technical interpretations
of the law.[42]

Much of Roosevelt's success as a politician, his prominence as
a reformer, his leading position as a progressive came from his
ability as a political journalist. He hammered out his phrases
with the skill of an experienced craftsman and the unceasing
energy of a prophet. The tone of his political writing is unmis-
takably that of confirmed righteousness. More than one critic
has written that he wrote always from the position of conviction.
He would attack and give no quarter. Although he is firm and
relentless, he is fair. He does not ridicule, nor is he sarcastic. His
nature and his personality require that he be ever a gentleman.
His expressions are as arresting and as innovative as was his
vision. For that reason his political writings are as fresh as they
were when he wrote them. Only repetition from time to time
mars his best efforts.

V The Books of World War I

America and the World War (1915)

When the World War began in Europe, Roosevelt became
the chief opponent of isolationism and pacifism, and published
America and the World War in 1915. Most of the articles had
previously appeared in the *New York Times* and other newspapers through the Wheeler Syndicate. No mission in Roosevelt's
life produced more vocal opponents, but he was willing to sac-

rifice his own reputation to prepare America to win the peace of righteousness. His chief adversary was President Woodrow Wilson.

In *America and the World War* Roosevelt makes no pretense that preparedness against war averts war any more than a fire department prevents fire; however, preparedness is the only hope in the event of war and the only salvation from disgrace. The examples of weak countries like Belgium and Luxembourg horrified him. China furnished another example of dismemberment by aggressors like Russia, Japan, Germany, France, and England. Never once would he retreat from the policy of the big stick, yet he constantly reiterates his personal abhorrence of war for its own sake. In the fashion of a Greek tale he volunteered his own life and that of his four sons for the cause of peace. The fervor of his words is meaningful only to the true believer: "If the only son who is killed at the front has no brother because his parents coldly dreaded to play their part in the Great Adventure of Life, then our sorrow is not for them, but solely for the son who himself dared the Great Adventure of Death. If, however, he is the only son because the Unseen Powers denied others to the love of his father and mother, then we mourn doubly with them because their darling went up to the sword of Azrael, because he drank the dark drink proffered by the Death Angel." [43]

All of Roosevelt's war essays are rich in historical allusions; and taken as the reflections of a working editorial writer during the events that led to our entry into the First World War, the essays remain a rich source of studious reflection for all time during periods of national danger. The ultrapacifist cannot save the country from disaster, and Roosevelt's main objective is to drown out his supine craving for peace at any price. Roosevelt believed in peace as much as any man; he even offered a comprehensive plan for a world league of peace in "Utopia or Hell?"; but he would not, under any circumstances, accept a peace that violated integrity or morality.

Fear God and Take Your Own Part (1916)

In *Fear God and Take Your Own Part* Roosevelt collected a series of items from various sources, but largely from *Metropolitan*. In an introductory note he acknowledges that most of his preaching in this book is repetitious. The themes of hyphenated

Americans, antipacifism and sentimentality, preparedness, and
our relations with Mexico dominate Roosevelt's interests in this
volume. Constantly his Aristotelian grasp of the two-sidedness
of things strikes the reader as an honest search for fairness.

Foes of Our Household (1917)

Although *Foes of Our Household* deals with domestic matters,
it is heavily colored by the events of World War I. The essays
attempt to provide guidance for the people at home to assist in
the winning of the war. The long delay in actually getting American men to the fronts irritated Roosevelt immensely. Germany's
strength had his respect, and as result urgency became the key-
note of his pleas for action. Repeatedly he draws the most sim-
plistic plans of action and divisions of labor. Plans and ideas for
the winning of the war come in every line. His fever pitch of enthusiasm never diminishes. In the movement at full speed he
seems to ignore the changes that had taken place in average
Americans; he underestimates their sophistication which com-
plicates the conduct of each successive war. Nothing at all is
wrong with Roosevelt's thought; it is merely that the country
had begun to outgrow him, for better or worse. His article on
"The Parasite Woman; the Only Indispensable Citizen" attests
to his tendency to be exactly right while at the same time over-
emphasizing the simplicity of the problem and its solution. He
summarizes his position: "But exactly as it is true that no nation
will prosper unless the average man is a home-maker; that is,
unless at some business or trade or profession, he earns enough
to make a home for himself and his wife and children, and is a
good husband and father; so no nation can exist at all unless the
average woman is the home-keeper, the good wife, and unless
she is the mother of a sufficient number of children to insure the
race going forward and not backward." [44] He admits that there
may be exceptional women who may not fit into this mould. Having made this admission, he loses the plainness of the problem to
complexity. Unfortunately, he falls into the camp of those who
see women as the producers of babies for national defense: "If
our birth-rate continues to diminish we shall by the end of this
century be impotent in the face of powers like Germany, Russia,
or Japan; we shall have been passed by the great states of South
America." [45]

The Great Adventure (1918)

Having influenced by his writing the entry of the United States into the war with Germany, Roosevelt sought with articles in the *Metropolitan Magazine* and the *Kansas City Star* to shape the terms of peace. His demands for unconditional surrender exerted considerable pressure on Wilson to pursue the war to an ultimate conclusion. Roosevelt's opposition to Wilson's "fourteen points" preceded his stronger objection to the plan for the League of Nations. In the opening sentences of *The Great Adventure,* a collection of articles on the aforementioned positions, Roosevelt's writing becomes as poetic as that of the Old Testament prophets:

Only those are fit to live who do not fear to die; and none are fit to die who have shrunk from the joy of life and the duty of life. Both life and death are parts of the same Great Adventure. Never yet was worthy adventure worthily carried through by the man who put his personal safety first. Never yet was a country worth living in unless its sons and daughters were of that stern stuff which bade them die for it at need; and never yet was a country worth dying for unless its sons and daughters thought of life not as something concerned only with the selfish evanescence of the individual, but as a link in the great chain of creation and causation, so that each person is seen in his true relations as an essential part of the whole, whose life must be made to serve the larger and continuing life of the whole.[46]

To the women he cries out: "Woe to those who invite a sterile death; a death not for them only, but for the race; the death which is insured by a life of sterile selfishness." [47] Then to the men again he says, "But honor, highest honor, to those who fearlessly face death for a good cause; no life is so honorable or so fruitful as such a death. Unless men are willing to fight and die for great ideals, including love of country, ideals will vanish, and the world will become one huge sty of materialism." [48] To Roosevelt, it would appear that nature supports the survival of the species and hardly that of the individual.

Roosevelt in *The Great Adventure* fights the war against Germany as fiercely as if he were in the trenches; nor does he spare Austria, Turkey, and Bulgaria, "Germany's three vassal allies." He sees Prussian society as aristocratic, capitalistic, and militaristic to the core, and adds that the guiding and ruling minority of that society has for centuries been saturated with the spirit of cynical and faithless brutality. On the other hand, his critiques of the situation in Russia and on Bolshevism, although accurate in their general statements, do not demonstrate any more than a superficial grasp of the true nature of Bolshevism.

The last portions of *The Great Adventure* warn against any premature peace. Roosevelt would not support, he says, any league of nations that was a substitute for our own military preparedness. His "War Aims and Peace Proposals" chapter contains a detailed attack on Wilson's "fourteen points" and remains a serious indictment of Wilson's instability in pursuing a just peace.

These World War I books were written by a Roosevelt possessed. Nothing he ever put on paper compares with them in intensity of purpose. Roosevelt was plainly the old warrior left at home. Considerable evidence in his correspondence and his article for *Outlook* on the death of Selous point up his great desire to die for the defense of his country in battle. Denied such a death, he lost himself in frustration, which translated into passionate appeals to his countrymen for a sacrifice he himself was not permitted by the War Department to make. The result was an inspired prose style that surpassed anything that he had previously achieved, but the content is limited to the age in which he was writing, or even the age before.

VI *The* Autobiography *(1913)*

Roosevelt's *Autobiography* plainly belongs among his journalistic writings. In February 1913 he began to publish in serial form in the *Outlook* "Chapters of a Possible Autobiography." He apparently had some difficulty in the writing of these chapters, which eventually were published as a book. He wrote to Emily Tyler Carow, his sister-in-law, on January 4, 1913: "I am having my hands full writing certain chapters of my past experiences. I have neglected *The Outlook* rather scandalously for a year and wanted to do something for them, and this was the only thing it seemed possible to do. But it is very difficult to strike just the happy mean between being too reticent and not reticent enough! I find it difficult both as regards my life when I was a child and my political experiences. I can only hope that I am handling it in a proper way." [49] Roosevelt never did really solve the problem, and the *Autobiography* is a severe disappointment to those familiar with his previous writings. One critic has said, "As long as a single copy of *An Autobiography* remains, it may judicially be said, Roosevelt's reputation as the apostle of the obvious is safe." [50]

Roosevelt repeats all too much, sometimes word for word, of what he previously said in other books. The greatest disappointment lies in the objectivity with which he writes. Of course this manner is consistent with his character, yet one feels that for once he might have revealed more of himself than he had previously—why he reached certain decisions, why he trusted or did not trust those around him, what were the alternatives in certain decisions, what mistakes had he made. As it is, the *Autobiography* is a mere recitation of events, told interestingly enough for anyone who has not read his other books. The "Chapters for a Possible Autobiography" show every evidence of being hastily accomplished for the next issue of *Outlook*. What is even more unfortunate, the *Autobiography* ends with the early months of 1909. Joseph L. Gardner, the author of *Departing Glory*, writes, "Thus, the Colonel remained uncharacteristically dispassionate and circumspect in writing his life, and the work—though it contains some charming chapters of his early years—is curiously unsatisfying." [51] There can be no doubt that the book, even taken as an objective recitation of events in Roosevelt's career, remains flawed more for what it excludes than for what it contains.

CHAPTER 5

Roosevelt as Writer

I *The Man*

WHO was the real Theodore Roosevelt? How can he be understood if the *Autobiography* helps but little? No less a perceptive person than William Dean Howells wrote to his brother, J. A. Howells, in 1906, "He is a strange man, and nobody has yet plucked out the heart of his mystery." [1] To understand Roosevelt, one must make his own conclusions from Roosevelt's writings. The *Literary Digest* once said of him, "Roosevelt is one of those authors who in their books unconsciously bare their soul. The French saying that the style is the man himself seems literal in this case." [2] One approach to Roosevelt's personality comes in focusing upon those qualities in his writings which reveal his boyish traits of enthusiasm, detachment, and intuition. Anyone can recognize the stunning power of the child that is paradoxically coupled with weakness in Roosevelt's character; this power is found in birds, animals, and other creatures of nature. [3] Roosevelt always projected this childlike side of his nature. Margaret Chanler in *Roman Spring* observed with accurate insight, "One of his charms lay in a certain boyish zest with which he welcomed everything that happened to him." [4] This childlike acceptance of every experience as a new experience can be achieved by very few men, yet it came to Roosevelt at Harvard, in a wet saddle out in North Dakota, and in the jungles of Brazil when nearly dead from insect bites and fever. Nicholas Murray Butler reiterated in *Across the Busy Years*, "As I have said, no man in my time has been so happy . . . ." [5] *Publishers' Weekly* paid the same respect to this trait in Roosevelt by saying, "For Theodore Roosevelt had that rare and priceless gift of remembering what it means to be a child; and of translating himself back for the hour, and understanding and sharing the interests of

143

his own children . . . ." [6] Finally, Stewart Edward White in reviewing Roosevelt's *Game Trails* observed, "He retains the boyish and delightful power of gloating over the strange and unusual. Without that power, which is only the power of 'make-believe' grown up, a man is middle-aged; with it he is always young." [7] Perhaps this trait in Roosevelt makes his *Letters to His Children* the best introduction to Roosevelt's biography and work. [8]

Those same energies that made Roosevelt appear childlike also brought his ability to throw himself into argument and controversy with complete abandon. No evidence exists anywhere in the mass of Roosevelt's writings that he is calling attention to himself. His detachment or disinterestedness derives from his ability to let his topic consume him. What often reaches the reader strongest is the aliveness of the man and the richness of his life. Nothing escapes his notice; everything is interesting when one truly sees. The hunt for a raccoon with children can be as real as the charge up a hill in Cuba if all of oneself is given to that moment. Then Roosevelt is speaking out of the very center of himself instinctively and intuitively. [9] Any critic of Roosevelt's time who was rooted in the rational could never understand him. H. L. Mencken, the acerbic essayist, did not know what to make of the intuitive actions of Roosevelt, and had to resort to using the word *instinctive* four times in his essay on Roosevelt. [10] Booker T. Washington in his own autobiography tells of Roosevelt's writing to him the day after taking office to invite Washington to the White House to discuss plans for helping the South which they had considered years before. Washington gives this careful description of Roosevelt's mind at work:

One of the most striking things about Mr. Roosevelt, both in private and public life, is his frankness. I have often been amazed at the absolute directness and candor of his speech. He does not seem to know how to hide anything. In fact, he seems to think aloud. Many people have referred to him as being impulsive and as acting without due consideration. From what I have seen of Mr. Roosevelt in this regard, I have reached the conclusion that what people describe as impulsiveness in him is nothing but quickness of thought. While other people are thinking around a question, he thinks through it. He reaches conclusions while other people are considering the preliminaries. He cut across the field, as it were, in his method of thinking. It is true that in doing so he often takes great chances and risks much.[11]

Henry Watterson, the editor, like Mencken failed to understand Roosevelt. He wrote in *Marse Henry*, "The inconsistencies and quarrels in which Theodore Roosevelt was now and again involved were largely temperamental. His mind was of an order which is prone to believe what it wants to believe. He did not take much time to think. He leaped at conclusions, and from his premise his conclusion was usually sound." [12] Similarly, William Lyon Phelps records in his *Autobiography with Letters* that William Howard Taft, even when Taft and Roosevelt were estranged, considered Roosevelt a man of genius, one of the greatest men he had ever known, and that Roosevelt always spoke impulsively without any regard as to possible consequences.[13] Henry A. Beers in a *Yale Review* article in 1919 stated:

Roosevelt, in fact, had no use for philosophy or speculative thought which could not be reduced to useful action. He was an eminently practical thinker. His mind was without subtlety, and he had little imagination. A life of thought for its own sake; the life of a dreamer or idealist; a life like that of Coleridge, with his paralysis of will and abnormal activity of the speculative faculty, eternally spinning metaphysical cobwebs, doubtless seemed to the author of "The Strenuous Life" a career of mere self-indulgence.[14]

Just as Associate Justice of the Supreme Court Benjamin N. Cordozo saw Roosevelt as a man "whose intuitions and perceptions were deep and brilliant," [15] a recent Secretary of State verifies the need for such gifts:

The dilemma of any statesman is that he can never be certain about the probable course of events. In reaching a decision, he must inevitably act on the basis of intuition that is inherently unprovable. If he insists on certainty, he runs the danger of becoming a prisoner of events. His resolution must reside not in "facts" as commonly conceived but in his vision of the future.[16]

Roosevelt had no programs or policies that grew from a broad philosophical structure; he operated out of the core of his being as each problem arose. In the same way, he wrote with gusto and abandon, just as a child throws himself into his play. And just as a child eschews sentimentality instinctively, unless conditioned to it by adults around him, Roosevelt found sentimentality to be a falseness utterly repugnant to him. Once called, with the possible exception of Mark Twain, the sturdiest opponent of sentimentality that America ever produced,[17] Roosevelt clearly had no such feeling in hunting animals, and never confused them with people. Yet this very lack of sentimentality in hunting, as in all things, was so tempered with sincerity and matter-of-factness that one reviewer said Roosevelt's books of hunting would have been just as delightful because of their detachment if he had been hunting Christian missionaries.[18] Time and again critics said that Roosevelt had no feelings. The fact is that he did not celebrate the subjective; he lived the life of objectivity and action. It is no wonder that his *Autobiography* reveals only indirectly Roosevelt's nature.

The value of Theodore Roosevelt's life and work can be found in his bravery, his love of nature, his childlike enthusiasm, his detachment, his zest for life: "The joy of living is his who has the heart to demand it."

II *Roosevelt's Place in Literature*

The character and adventures of Theodore Roosevelt have marked his writings in such a way that even his style reflects the man of action, the man of combativeness, and the man of righteousness. Roosevelt had the gifts of lucidity and directness in his books that reflect the man's sincerity more than anything else about him. Hardly a sentence in his publications cannot be understood on the first reading. Out of his personality came the urgent need to make himself immediately understood. His rampant enthusiasm demanded the plain and instantaneous transmission of his meaning. Coherence and emphasis were never problems for him. The pitfalls into which he often stumbled, instead, were those of redundancy and repetition. The *Bookman* of October 1919 offers a succinct summary of his defects: "His style, though always lucid and forcible, was variable. He had certain faults—he was often redundant; at times he used too many words, and repeated himself too often. But oddly enough, his redundancy rarely interfered with clearness, as it did not put things out of proportion, nor change the relative importance of his topics; and his repetitions had the effect of overemphasis rather than of paucity of thought." [19]

Anyone who writes as much as Roosevelt wrote will reveal some shortcomings in his work. Sooner or later someone will pounce upon such ample defects, as did the *Independent* of October 9, 1913, in concentrating on Roosevelt's frequent repetition, his unrestricted tendency to indulge in exhortation, his occasional extravagance of statement, and more than occasional looseness of structure. Yet the same review concludes that "the spirit that pervades every page is that of high altruism coupled with an unquenchable zeal for life." [20] The same close identity of Roosevelt's character and books appears in the *Bulletin of the Society of American Authors* of 1901 with a quotation from the *Times*: "In his histories and biographies, Roosevelt the writer is most successful when Roosevelt the man is completely enlisted, and when his subject is of the sort to which his multiform activities have been most closely related. They are best, certainly they are most interesting, where they are the unconscious representation of the suthor's mind and character." [21]

Robert Bridges, his editor at Scribner's, who knew him better as an author than most of his contemporaries, attests to Roosevelt's rapid composition in preparing his manuscripts. After speaking of Roosevelt's painstaking efforts in Africa and Brazil in producing copy under difficult conditions, Bridges relates:

In civilized countries the Colonel generally dictated his articles and books, but made a most thorough revision of the typewritten copy. The stenographer who took his dictation for *Oliver Cromwell,* when Roosevelt was Governor, said that he would appear in his study with some books of reference and a pad of memoranda. Then he would start to dictate, and with hardly a pause would complete a chapter of historical narrative which demanded a very careful knowledge of dates and places. This was not so easy as a narrative of personal experience. Nevertheless, I once read a chapter of it before the Colonel had seen the stenographer's transcript. It could have been printed as it stood with mere mechanical proofreading corrections.[22]

Unquestionably such an irregular manner of producing a book might better serve an improviser of poems such as Lord Byron, who could meet the requirements of form in a Spenserian stanza to produce *Childe Harold's Pilgrimage,* and is not suited to the careful demands of fine style in a more loosely structured essay. Although early in his career Roosevelt lamented his failure at achieving grace in his written work, he soon abandoned any efforts and resigned himself to producing clear, direct, forceful prose. It would be unfair to Roosevelt to dismiss his achievements too casually as insufficient. There were times when he could find satisfaction in his work. When asked to choose the best passages in his writings, he selected certain paragraphs from his *Autobiography*, the first ten pages of *The Winning of the West*, portions of *Progressive Principles*, and many pages from his hunting books and presidential papers and addresses.[23] When not prolix, Roosevelt's prose demonstrates a significant level of achievement. George William Douglas in *The Many-Sided Roosevelt* gives an interesting view of Roosevelt's writing from the other side of the Atlantic:

Out of his reading and deep thinking there has come an intellectual attitude and a literary style that rests on the foundation of the best that has been said and done. An interesting and significant commentary on that style and that state of mind was made by Mr. R. J. Walker of St. Paul's School, West Kensington, in a letter to the London *Times* commenting on the President's inaugural address of March 4, 1905. Mr. Walker wrote: "May I crave space to call attention to the extraordinary resemblance in spirit between President Roosevelt's inaugural oration and the speeches of Pericles in the second book of Thucydides? I doubt whether there is a sentence in the English which can not be paralleled in the Greek, as regards meaning at least, and often as regards form. I set to-day a section of the oration for translation into Greek prose, and I asked our head form, 'Where does this English come from?' The general answer was, 'From Jowett's translation of Thucydides.' " [24]

Essentially a politician first and a writer only when time was available, Roosevelt has left a lasting impression of his talent as an author. Charles Ferguson in his essay "Roosevelt—Man of Letters" laments that Roosevelt was a man of remarkable literary talent who remains known chiefly for his political activity. Ferguson sees much more in Roosevelt as a writer:

What I want to suggest is that, apart from being a patriot and a Republican, Roosevelt bore the hallmark of a genuine man of letters and, had he devoted his life altogether to composition, he would have gained for himself a position in American literature equaled by few other men. That the excessive activity superinduced by his political interests prohibited the fullest development of his talents is of course obvious from a reading of his later writings. But the fact remains that, with all his outside duties, Roosevelt slung a wicked pen, and he rates distinction for his excellent writing as well as for his handling of some questions of world importance.[25]

Roosevelt's books can be found in libraries from Freiburg to Tokyo; most of his books have remained in print, and several have recently been reissued in new editions. His nature books still rank among the best of their kind because of the author's gift of accurate observation. His histories and biographies will always provide an original point of view marked by Roosevelt's own character. His letters and *Autobiography* serve to demonstrate his sizeable contributions to the arts in America and his influence in all areas of national life. His political writings are indispensable to the history of reform movements in the United States. True, he is a moralist and a preacher, "but surely he is a preacher with a grasp on the history of man and of nature not often paralleled, with a practical experience of life given to but few, with a sportsman's exhilaration in movement and adventure, with an artist's eye for the concrete and picturesque, and, finally with an uncloistered style capable of carrying his thoughts and feelings straight to the mind and heart of every reader . . . ." [26] The anonymous commentator for the *Independent* who wrote these words continues, "but whether he discusses problems of government as a statesman, or social evils as a reformer, or literature as a wide reader, he is always the man of singularly open sympathies, of large views, of copious information, and in the main, of catholic and balanced judgment." [27]

Even if Roosevelt's books disappear from the shelves of the world's libraries, his place in literature is secure. As President, Roosevelt served more than any man in American history to give a new spirit to American letters. His habit of encouraging authors in their work and his constant habit of inviting them to the White House and making them his friends have included his name in the biographies of every author of his time. Alfred Kazin in *On Native Grounds,* a splendid study that covers the period of Roosevelt's influence, states categorically that with the coming of Roosevelt a new spirit of active and critical realism swept through politics and journalism and "gave a new impetus to young realistic novelists and stimulated American liberal thought in every sphere." [28] Roosevelt with his moral leadership and genuine interest in fellow authors brought American literature grandly into the twentieth century.

Notes and References

Chapter One

1. Corinne Roosevelt Robinson, *My Brother Theodore Roosevelt* (New York, 1921), pp. 4, 9.
2. Peleg Dennis Harrison, *The Stars and Stripes and Other American Flags* (Boston, 1908), pp. 365–66. The number on the house was changed from 33 to 28 in 1867.
3. Robinson, p. 4.
4. Richard Welling, *As the Twig Is Bent* (New York, 1924), p. 103.
5. Theodore Roosevelt, *Diaries of Boyhood and Youth* (New York, 1928), p. 99.
6. Theodore Roosevelt, *An Autobiography, The Works of Theodore Roosevelt,* National Edition, 20 volumes (New York, 1926), XX, 20 (hereafter cited as *Works*).
7. Ibid., p. 24.
8. For a thorough Freudian interpretation of Roosevelt's early childhood and predictable inferences, see Glenn Davis, "The Early Years of Theodore Roosevelt: A Study in Character Formation," *History of Childhood Quarterly: The Journal of Psychohistory* 2:4 (Spring 1975): 461–92 and 3:1 (Summer 1974): 43–74. For a more conventional study of the early years, see Carleton Putnam, *Theodore Roosevelt, The Formative Years, 1858–1866* (New York, 1958).
9. Welling, p. 32.
10. *Theodore Roosevelt Papers* (Washington, D.C., 1969), Series 8, January 2, 1878. The diaries which Roosevelt kept while at Harvard College are in Series 8, reels 429–30 of the 485 reels of microfilm that comprise the *Presidential Papers* of Roosevelt, hereafter cited as *Papers.* (Citations for the entries in the Harvard diary and other diaries are omitted because they can readily be gleaned from the dates in the text and located in the *Papers.*)
11. H. W. Thompson, "Theodore Roosevelt," *State College Quarterly* 4 (June 1919): 8.

12. Welling, p. 32.
13. *Papers,* Series 8, September 14, 1881.
14. See Willard B. Gatewood, Jr., *Theodore Roosevelt and the Art of Controversy* (Baton Rouge, 1970), p. 7.
15. Roosevelt to Washburn, November 10, 1881, *The Letters of Theodore Roosevelt,* ed. Elting E. Morison, 8 vols. (Cambridge, Mass., 1951–1954), I, 55. (hereafter cited as *Letters*).
16. Roosevelt to Anna Roosevelt, September 15, 1882, *Letters,* I, 57.
17. George M. Frederickson, *The Inner Civil War* (New York, 1965), pp. 224–25.
18. Theodore Roosevelt, *In Memory of My Darling Wife* (New York, n.d.), p. 3.
19. Ibid., p. 5.
20. Theodore Roosevelt Collection, Harvard College Library.
21. Roosevelt to Simon Newton Dexter North, April 30, 1884, *Letters,* I, 66.
22. Roosevelt to Henry Cabot Lodge, March 27, 1886, *Letters,* I, 95.
23. Welling, p. 52.
24. Roosevelt to Lodge, August 24, 1884, *Letters,* I, 80.
25. Roosevelt to Corinne Roosevelt Robinson, February 8, 1887, *Letters,* I, 121.
26. Roosevelt to Lodge, July 1, 1889, *Letters,* I, 168.
27. Roosevelt to Lodge, July 6, 1889, *Letters,* I, 169.
28. The manuscript bibliography of Robert W. G. Vail in the *Theodore Roosevelt Collection* is indispensable in tracing the publications of Theodore Roosevelt.
29. Roosevelt to Kruse, April 6, 1891, *Letters,* I, 241.
30. Stefan Lorant, *The Life and Times of Theodore Roosevelt* (New York, 1959), p. 498.
31. Roosevelt to Matthews, June 29, 1894, *Letters,* I, 389.
32. Ibid., p. 390.
33. Roosevelt to Matthews, June 8, 1893, *Letters,* I, 320.
34. Roosevelt to Anna Roosevelt, December 17, 1893, *Letters,* I, 343.
35. Roosevelt to Levi Parsons Morton, March 19, 1895, *Letters,* I, 436.
36. Roosevelt, *An Autobiography, Works,* XX, 174.
37. Jean Holloway, *Hamlin Garland* (Austin, 1960), p. 131.
38. Paul Russel Cutright, *Theodore Roosevelt the Naturalist* (New York, 1956), pp. 84–85.
39. Roosevelt to Trent, February 23, 1898, *Letters,* I, 782.
40. Roosevelt to Bates, September 29, 1897, *Letters,* I, 694.

41. Ibid.
42. Roosevelt to Wister, December 13, 1897, *Letters*, I, 742.
43. Roosevelt to Cecil Arthur Spring Rice, May 29, 1897, *Letters*, I, 618–21.
44. Roosevelt to Long, March 25, 1898, *Letters*, I, 799.
45. Roosevelt to Bradley Tyler Johnson, March 7, 1898, *Letters*, I, 789.
46. Roosevelt to Dana, April 18, 1898, *Letters*, II, 816.
47. Roosevelt to Brooks Brothers, May 2, 1898, *Letters*, II, 822.
48. Roosevelt to Steffens, May 4, 1898, *Letters*, II, 823.
49. Roosevelt to Corrine Roosevelt Robinson, June 7, 1898, *Letters*, I, 836.
50. Roosevelt to Corinne Roosevelt Robinson, June 15, 1898, *Letters*, II, 845.
51. Roosevelt to Lodge, January 12, 1899, *Letters*, II, 909.
52. Roosevelt to Trevelyan, January 16, 1899, *Letters*, II, 914.
53. Roosevelt to Henderson, February 14, 1899, *Letters*, II, 945.
54. Roosevelt to Whitney, August 3, 1899, *Letters*, II, 1044.
55. Roosevelt to W. E. Warner, February 1, 1900, *Letters*, II, 1158.
56. Roosevelt to Dunne, November 28, 1899, *Letters*, II, 1099.
57. Roosevelt to Rideing, April 20, 1901, *Letters*, III, 61.
58. Roosevelt to Wister, July 20, 1901, *Letters*, III, 127.
59. Maurice Francis Egan, *Recollections of a Happy Life* (New York, 1924), p. 209.
60. Broadus F. Farrar, "John Burroughs, Theodore Roosevelt and the Nature-Fakers," *Tennessee Studies in Literature* 4, (1959): 121–30.
61. Vail manuscript.
62. Ibid.
63. Morison, VII, 77.
64. Roosevelt to Robinson, October 19, 1910, *Letters*, VI, 145.
65. Morison, VII, 654.
66. Roosevelt to F. D. Roosevelt, May 10, 1913, *Letters*, VII, 729.
67. Roosevelt to Frank Michler Chapman, November 4, 1913, *Letters*, VII, 754.
68. "The Week," *Outlook*, July 11, 1914, p. 570.
69. Roosevelt to Chanler, March 12, 1915, *Letters*, VIII, 908–909.
70. For one account of the army's point of view see Hugh L. Scott, *Some Memoirs of a Soldier* (New York, 1928).
71. Roosevelt to White, February 17, 1917, *Letters*, VIII, 1153.
72. Roosevelt to Wharton, August 15, 1918, *Letters*, VIII, 1363.
73. Mary Roberts Rinehart, *My Story* (New York, 1931), pp. 241, 259.

Chapter Two

1. John Higham, *History* (New Jersey, 1965), p. 4.
2. Ibid., p. 148.
3. Ibid., p. 6.
4. Roosevelt, *The Naval War of 1812, Works,* VI, 428.
5. Ibid., pp 152–53.
6. Ibid., p. xxiv.
7. Ibid., p. 122.
8. Ibid., p. 168.
9. Ibid., p. 275.
10. Ibid., p. 157.
11. Ibid., p. 174.
12. Ibid., p. 223.
13. "Our Navy in 1812," *New York Times,* June 5, 1882, p. 3, col. 1.
14. "An American Historian of the British Navy," *Macmillan's Magazine* 78 (1898): 13.
15. Ibid., p. 22.
16. Roosevelt, *The Naval War of 1812, Works,* VI, 383.
17. Ibid., p. 394.
18. "The Naval War of 1812," *New York Times,* October 28, 1883, p. 12, col. 3.
19. [William Frederick Poole], "Roosevelt's *The Winning of the West," Atlantic Monthly* 64 (1889): 694.
20. Higham, p. 150.
21. "Pushing Their Way," *New York Times,* July 7, 1889, p. 11, col. 4.
22. Roosevelt, *The Winning of the West, Works,* VIII, 101.
23. Ibid., p. 120.
24. Ibid., p. 71.
25. George B. Utley, "Theodore Roosevelt's *The Winning of the West*: Some Unpublished Letters," *Mississippi Valley Historical Review* 30 (1944): 495.
26. Ibid., p. 499.
27. Ibid., p. 501.
28. Ibid., p. 503.
29. Ibid., pp. 504–505.
30. Morison, II, 1099.
31. Roosevelt, *The Rough Riders, Works,* XI, 36.
32. Ibid., pp. 39–40.
33. Ibid., p. 60.
34. Ibid., p. 61.
35. Ibid., p. 63.
36. For a laudatory eye-witness account of the performance of the

Rough Riders see John H. Parker, *History of the Gatling Gun Detachment Fifth Army Corps, at Santiago, with a Few Untarnished Truths Concerning that Expedition* (Kansas City, Mo., 1898).

37. Roosevelt, *Thomas Hart Benton, Works,* VII, 204.
38. Ibid., p. 136.
39. Ibid., p. 41.
40. Ibid., p. 60.
41. Ibid., p. 83.
42. Ibid., pp. 79–80.
43. Ibid., p. 121.
44. Ibid., p. 220.
45. Ibid., p. 163.
46. Ibid., p. 48.
47. Ibid., p. 62.
48. Ibid., p. 64.
49. Ibid., p. 216.
50. Ibid., p. 233.
51. "Mr. Roosevelt's *Benton,*" *New York Times,* May 15, 1887, p. 4, col. 2.
52. Roosevelt, *Gouverneur Morris, Works,* VII, 469–70.
53. Ibid., p. 278.
54. Ibid., pp. 421–22.
55. Ibid., p. 397.
56. Roosevelt, *Thomas Hart Benton, Works,* VII, 50.
57. Roosevelt, *Gouverneur Morris, Works,* VII, 461.
58. Ibid., pp. 406–407.
59. Ibid., p. 328.
60. Ibid., p. 329.
61. Ibid., p. 328.
62. Roosevelt, *Oliver Cromwell, Works,* X, 288.
63. Ibid., p. 226.
64. Ibid., p. 190.
65. Ibid., p. 209.
66. Ibid.
67. Ibid., p. 316.
68. Ibid., p. 243.
69. Ralph C. H. Catterall, "Some Recent Literature on Oliver Cromwell," Bibliographical Society of Chicago *Yearbook 1900–01,* p. 42.
70. Ibid.
71. "Three Cromwell Books," *Antiquary* 37(1901): 19.
72. Ibid.
73. "Cromwell," *New York Times Saturday Review of Books and Art* 5 (1900): 674.
74. Roosevelt, *New York, Works,* X, 359.

75. Ibid., pp. 367–68.
76. Ibid., pp. 485–86.
77. Ibid., p. 498.
78. Ibid., p. 519.
79. Ibid., p. 524.
80. Ibid., p. 530.
81. Ibid., p. 537.
82. "Historic New York," *New York Times,* March 29, 1891, p. 19, col. 4.
83. Ibid., col. 4.
84. Roosevelt, *Men of Action, Works,* XI, 206.
85. Ibid., p. 210.
86. Ibid., p. 246.
87. Ibid., p. 265.
88. Roosevelt, *Hero Tales from American History, Works,* X, 97.
89. Samuel Eliot Morison, "History as a Literary Art," *Harvard Guide to American History,* rev. ed., ed. Frank Freidel (Cambridge, Mass., 1974), I, 3–4.
90. Ibid., p. 4.
91. Allen Nevins, *Allen Nevins on History* (New York, 1975), p. 284.

Chapter Three

1. In an editorial of February 25, 1878, the *New York Evening Post* reported a meeting of an ornithological club in Cambridge, Mass., at which Theodore Roosevelt offered his views on the usefulness of the American sparrow.
2. John M. Blum, "Theodore Roosevelt: The Years of Decision," *The Letters of Theodore Roosevelt,* II, 1484–94.
3. Ibid., p. 1486.
4. Roosevelt, *Hunting Trips of a Ranchman, Works,* I, 93.
5. Ibid., p. 191.
6. "Books," *Spectator* 59 (1886): 82.
7. "New Publications," *Forest and Stream* 24 (1885): 451.
8. "New Publications," *New York Times,* July 13, 1885, p. 3, col. 1.
9. Roosevelt, *Ranch Life and the Hunting Trail, Works,* I, 269.
10. Ibid., pp. 273–74.
11. Ibid., p. 274.
12. Ibid., pp. 280–81.
13. Ibid., p. 281.
14. Ibid., p. 290.
15. Ibid., p. 293.
16. Ibid., p. 325.

17. Ibid., p. 353.
18. Ibid., pp. 364–65.
19. Ibid., p. 368.
20. Ibid., p. 375.
21. Roosevelt, *The Wilderness Hunter, Works,* II, 357.
22. "Mr. Roosevelt's Americanism," *New York Times,* August 6, 1893, p. 19, col. 3.
23. Ibid.
24. [J. H. Porter], "The Wilderness Hunter," *Atlantic Monthly* 75 (1895): 827.
25. "Roosevelt's Outdoor Pastimes of an American Hunter," *Harvard Graduates' Magazine* 14 (1906): 412.
26. Roosevelt, *Outdoor Pastimes of an American Hunter, Works,* III, 112.
27. Ibid., pp. 122–23.
28. Roosevelt collaborated with the naturalist Edmund Heller and produced a scientific two volume work: *Life Histories of African Game Animals* (New York, 1914).
29. George Bird Grinnell, "Roosevelt in Africa," *American Review of Reviews* 42 (1910): 461.
30. Harold Hayes, "The Curtain Falls on the Great White Hunter," *Travel and Leisure* 4: 12 (1974): 27.
31. Ibid.
32. Roosevelt, *African Game Trails, Works,* IV, 88.
33. Joan London, *Jack London and His Times* (Seattle, 1968), p. 284.
34. See George E. Mowry, *The Era of Theodore Roosevelt* (New York, 1958), pp. 92–93.
35. Roosevelt, *African Game Trails, Works,* IV, xxiii.
36. Ibid., xxiv–xxv.
37. "The Colonel and His Book," *Bookman* 32: 2 (1910): 113.
38. Ibid., pp. 112–13.
39. Roosevelt, *Through the Brazilian Wilderness, Works,* V, 9.
40. "Book News and Reviews," *Bird-Lore* 17: 1 (1915): 49.
41. Roosevelt, *Through the Brazilian Wilderness, Works,* V, 247.
42. George K. Cherrie, *Address,* Explorer's Club, March 1, 1919.
43. John W. Evans, "The Roosevelt-Rondon Expedition," *Geographical Journal* 45 (1915): 154.
44. Roosevelt, *Through the Brazilian Wilderness, Works,* V, 15.
45. Ibid., p. 28.
46. Ibid., p. 29.
47. Ibid., pp. 119–20.
48. Roosevelt, *A Book-Lover's Holidays in the Open, Works,* III, 183.
49. Ibid., p. 331.

50. Ibid., p. 342.
51. Ibid., p. 347.
52. Farrar, pp. 121–30.
53. Roosevelt, *Papers on Natural History, Works,* V, 389.
54. Ibid., p. 390.
55. Ibid., p. 393.

Chapter Four

1. Gerald F. Else, *The Origin and Early Form of Greek Tragedy* (New York, 1972), p. 39.
2. Ibid., pp. 39–40.
3. Ibid., p. 48.
4. William Allen White, "Saith the Preacher!" Roosevelt, *Works* XII, 68.
5. Philip Appleman, ed., *Darwin* (New York, 1970), pp. 512–19.
6. Roosevelt, *Literary Essays, Works,* XII, 68.
7. Ibid., p. 69.
8. Ibid., p. 73.
9. Ibid., p. 85.
10. Ibid., p. 86.
11. Ibid., p. 93.
12. Ibid., p. 107.
13. Ibid., p. 112.
14. Ibid., p. 113.
15. Ibid., p. 121.
16. Ibid., p. 123.
17. Ibid., p. 130.
18. Ibid., p. 147.
19. "Shaw vs. Roosevelt on Birth Control," *Physical Culture* 52: 3 (1924): 33–34, 72, 74, 78–80.
20. *Papers,* Series 1, February 25, 1905.
21. Roosevelt, *American Ideals, Works,* XIII, 289.
22. Ibid., p. 23.
23. Ibid., p. 161.
24. Ibid., p. 4.
25. Ibid., p. 211.
26. Ibid., p. 195.
27. Ibid., p. 45.
28. George Merriam Hyde, "Adventures in Criticism," *Bookman* 6 (1898): 466.
29. Roosevelt, *American Ideals, Works,* XIII, xvii.
30. Roosevelt, *The Strenuous Life, Works,* XIII, 572.
31. Ibid., p. 470.
32. Ibid., p. 477.

33. Ibid., p. 554.

34. Roosevelt, *Campaigns and Controversies, Works,* XIV, 322.

35. Ibid., p. 196.

36. Walter Neale, *Life of Ambrose Bierce* (New York, 1929), p. 108.

37. M. A. De Wolfe Howe, *Barrett Wendell and His Letters* (Boston, 1924), p. 251.

38. Roosevelt, *State Papers as Governor and Presidential Addresses, Works,* XV, 4.

39. Benjamin N. Cardozo, *The Nature of the Judicial Process* (New Haven, 1921), p. 171.

40. "Has the Supreme Court Abandoned the Constitution?" *Saturday Review* May 28, 1977.

41. James William Hurst, *The Growth of American Law* (Boston, 1950), p. 32.

42. The reform activities of Roosevelt really do not come within the aims of this book. However, I must point out that *Social Justice and Popular Rule* contains Roosevelt's radical "Osawatomie Speech," titled "The New Nationalism." For a detailed discussion of the New Nationalism, see Charles Forcey, *The Crossroads of Liberalism: Croly, Weyl, Lippmann and the Progressive Era, 1900–1925* (New York, 1961); also see Forcey's "Introduction" in Herbert Croly, *The Promise of American Life* (New York, 1963).

43. Roosevelt, *The Great Adventure, Works,* XIX, 246.

44. Roosevelt, *Foes of Our Household, Works,* XIX, 142–43.

45. Ibid., p. 159.

46. Roosevelt, *The Great Adventure, Works,* XIX, 243.

47. Ibid., p. 245.

48. Ibid.

49. Roosevelt to Carow, January 4, 1913, *Letters,* VII, 689.

50. Hamilton Basso, *Mainstream* (New York, 1943), p. 164.

51. Joseph L. Gardner, *Departing Glory* (New York, 1973), p. 284.

Chapter Five

1. William D. Howells, *Life in Letters of William Dean Howells,* ed. Mildred Howells (Garden City, 1928), II, 220.

2. "Col. Roosevelt's Holidays in the Open," *Literary Digest* 52 (1916): 1290.

3. For these insights into Roosevelt's character I am most indebted to R. H. Blyth, *Zen in English Literature and Oriental Classics* (New York, 1960).

4. Margaret Chanler, *Roman Spring* (Boston, 1934), pp. 195–96.

5. Nicholas Murray Butler, *Across the Busy Years* (New York, 1939), pp. 416–17.

6. Frederick Taber Cooper, "An Intimate Aspect of Roosevelt," *Publishers' Weekly*, September 20, 1919, p. 750.

7. Stewart Edward White, "Nine Books of the Month," *Bookman* 32 (1910): 171.

8. Roosevelt, *Theodore Roosevelt's Letters to His Children, Works*, XIX, 409–551.

9. Intuitive thought has always been associated with the feminine mind, as in Karl Stern, *The Flight from Woman* (New York, 1965); consequently, the comments of several authors on the feminine in Roosevelt should be of interest: Duffield Osborne, "Roosevelt: A Feminine Type," *Forum* 43 (1910): 198; George Sylvester Viereck, *Roosevelt: A Study in Ambivalence* (New York, 1919), pp. 62–63; William Allen White, *Masks in a Pageant* (New York, 1928), p. 285.

10. Henry Louis Mencken, *Prejudices: A Second Series* (New York, 1920), pp. 102–35.

11. Booker T. Washington, *My Larger Education* (New York, 1920), p. 167.

12. Henry Watterson, *Marse Henry* (New York, 1919), p. 167.

13. William Lyon Phelps, *Autobiography with Letters* (New York, 1939), p. 608.

14. Henry A. Beers, *Four Americans* (New Haven, 1920), pp. 12–13.

15. Cardozo, p. 171.

16. Henry A. Kissinger, "Reflections on Cuba," *Reporter*, November 22, 1962, p. 21.

17. Thompson, p. 5.

18. Charles W. Ferguson, "Roosevelt—Man of Letters," *Bookman* 64 (1927): 727.

19. "The Gossip Shop," *Bookman* 50 (1919): 248.

20. "Mr. Roosevelt as Essayist," *Independent*, October 9, 1913, p. 93.

21. *Bulletin of the Society of American Authors* 6:11 (1901): 331.

22. Robert Bridges, *Roosevelt as We Knew Him*, ed. Frederick S. Wood (Philadelphia, 1927), p. 315.

23. Charles Grenfill Washburn, *Harvard Graduates' Magazine* 27 (1919): 474–77.

24. George William Douglas, *The Many-Sided Roosevelt* (New York, 1907), pp. 183–84.

25. Charles W. Ferguson, "Roosevelt—Man of Letters," *Bookman* 64 (1927): 726.

26. "Mr. Roosevelt as Essayist," p. 93.

27. Ibid.

28. Alfred Kazin, *On Native Grounds* (Garden City, 1956), p. 69.

Selected Bibliography

Bibliographical note: The first serious attempt at a bibliography of Roosevelt's works was compiled by Joseph B. Gilder for the *New York Times* of October 19, 1901. The bibliography was brief, yet Gilder remarked in his introduction, "As a habitual pursuit, stone-breaking must, by comparison, seem a frivolous occupation." R. W. G. Vail commented further, "His successors in the same field will most assuredly agree with Mr. Gilder." The manuscript bibliography, prepared by Robert W. G. Vail of the Theodore Roosevelt Collection at the Harvard College Library is the most complete version of Roosevelt's publications. The most useful general bibliography of Roosevelt's works and works about him and works that depict his time can be found in the Harvard University Library publication *Theodore Roosevelt Collection*, in five volumes, distributed by the Harvard University Press since 1970. The compilation includes twenty-three bibliographies of Roosevelt's publications. An abbreviated version of the *Theodore Roosevelt Collection* can be found in Edward Wagenknecht's *The Seven Worlds of Theodore Roosevelt*. Other comprehensive bibliographies can be found in *The Era of Theodore Roosevelt*, by George E. Mowry, and *Power and Responsibility*, by William Henry Harbaugh. The presidential *Papers* have been microfilmed and distributed to major libraries throughout the United States; they have a useful index system which amounts to a bibliography.

PRIMARY SOURCES

The Works of Theodore Roosevelt. National Edition, 20 vols. New York: Charles Scribner's Sons. 1926. I. *Hunting Trips of a Ranchman; Ranch Life and the Hunting Trail*. II. *The Wilderness Hunter; Outdoor Pastimes of an American Hunter*. III. *Outdoor Pastimes of an American Hunter* (Concluded); *A Book-Lover's Holidays in the Open*. IV. *African Game Trails* V. *Through the Brazilian Wilderness; Papers on Natural History*. VI *The Naval War of 1812*. VII. *Thomas Hart Benton; Gouverneur Morris*. VIII. *The Winning of the West*. IX. *The Winning of the West* (Concluded). X. *Hero Tales from American History; Oliver Cromwell; New York.* XI. *The Rough Riders; Men of Action.* XII. *Literary Essays.* XIII. *American Ideals; The Strenuous Life; Realizable Ideals.* XIV. *Campaigns and Controversies.* XV. *State Papers as Governor and President.* XVI. *American Problems.* XVII. *Social Justice and Popular Rule.* XVIII. *America and the World War; Fear God and Take Your Own Part.* XIX. *The Foes of Our Own Household; The Great Adventure; Letters to His Children.* XX. *An Autobiography.*

The Works of Theodore Roosevelt. Memorial Edition, 24 vols. New York: Charles Scribner's Sons, 1923–26. A comparison of the contents of the National Edition and the Memorial Edition can be found in the *Theodore Roosevelt Cyclopedia,* pp. x–xi.

Presidential Addresses and State Papers; European Addresses. Homeward Bound Edition, 8 vols. New York: The Review of Reviews Co., 1910.

The Letters of Theodore Roosevelt. 8 vols. Ed. Elting E. Morison. Cambridge: Harvard Univ. Press, 1951–54.

Theodore Roosevelt Papers. 485 reels, microfilm. Washington, D.C.: Library of Congress, 1969.

Diaries of Boyhood and Youth. New York: Charles Scribner's Sons, 1928.

Selections from the Correspondence of Theodore Roosevelt and Henry Cabot Lodge, 1884–1918. 2 vols. New York: Charles Scribner's Sons, 1925.

Theodore Roosevelt and His Time, Shown in His Own Letters. 2 vols. Ed. Joseph B. Bishop. New York: Charles Scribner's Sons, 1920.

Roosevelt in the Kansas City Star; War-time Editorials by Theodore Roosevelt. Ed. Ralph Stout. Boston: Houghton Mifflin Co., 1921.

Letters from Theodore Roosevelt to Anna Roosevelt Cowles, 1870–1918. New York: Charles Scribner's Sons, 1924.

Letters to Kermit. Ed. Will Irwin. New York: Charles Scribner's Sons, 1946.

Theodore Roosevelt Cyclopedia. Eds. Albert Bushnell Hart and Herbert Ronald Ferleger. New York: Roosevelt House, 1941.

SECONDARY SOURCES

If there really are more stars in the heavens than there are grains of sand on all the beaches of all the world, then their number can be rivaled by the seemingly infinite number of allusions to Roosevelt in the memoirs, autobiographies, biographies, and letters of his time. Any name in this book will lead to materials. The *New York Times* index and the periodical indexes provide indications to the reviews of his books, as does the *Book Review Digest.* Very little has been written about Roosevelt as an author and critic. The *Outlook* contains most of the long book reviews which he wrote. The four indexes in Morison's *Letters of Theodore Roosevelt* have a prodigious number of useful entries under "Authors." Listed below are items that might prove of use for further study of Roosevelt's intellectual life.

ANONYMOUS. "The Writings of Theodore Roosevelt." *Book Buyer* 18:1 (1899): 5–9. A review of Roosevelt's books to 1899. Finds some disappointments in Roosevelt's hasty writing and questions the validity of the position "America, right or wrong."

BASSO, HAMILTON. *Mainstream.* New York: Reynal & Hitchcock, 1943. A bittersweet evaluation of Roosevelt's intellectual personality, written with verve.

BUSCH, NOEL F. *T.R.: The Story of Theodore Roosevelt and His Influence on Our Times.* New York: Reynal & Company, 1963. Recognizes that Roosevelt was an author, spoke about authors, and that authors spoke about him. In other words, Busch sees Roosevelt as more than a politician.

CHERRIE, GEORGE K. *Dark Trails, Adventures of a Naturalist.* New York: G. P. Putnam's Sons, 1930. Tells much of the personal heroism Roosevelt showed on his perilous adventure through Brazil. Roosevelt himself gave fewer details of the suffering the party endured.

CORDINGLEY, NORA E. "Extreme Rarities in the Published Works of Theodore Roosevelt." *Papers of the Bibliographical Society of America* 39 (1945): 20–50. Especially useful for Roosevelt's ornithological works.

FERGUSON, CHARLES W. "Roosevelt—Man of Letters." *Bookman* 64 (1927): 726–29. Review of the National Edition of Roosevelt's *Works;* finds some of the volumes disappointing but insists that Roosevelt has importance as a literary figure.

GARDNER, JOSEPH L. *Departing Glory: Theodore Roosevelt as Ex-President.* New York: Charles Scribner's Sons, 1973. Although Gardner is primarily interested in Roosevelt's political life, he does give much attention to Roosevelt with the *Outlook,* the *Kansas City Star,* and *Metropolitan.*

GATEWOOD, WILLARD B. *Theodore Roosevelt and the Art of Controversy.* Baton Rouge: Louisiana State Univ. Press, 1970. The chapter on "The Struggle for an Artistic Coinage" accurately depicts the resistance Roosevelt met in some of his artistic interests.

GERSON, NOEL B. *TR.* Garden City: Doubleday & Company, Inc., 1970. This biographical novel has been adequately researched and provides an excellent introduction to many facets of Roosevelt's life.

GILDER, JOSEPH B. "A Man of Letters in the White House." *Critic* 29

(1901): 401–409. One of the earliest articles to give full attention to the broad aspects of Roosevelt's literary life and writings.

KAZIN, ALFRED. *On Native Grounds.* Garden City: Doubleday Anchor
Books, 1956. The first third of this book is still the best survey of
American prose literature during the period that Roosevelt was
writing. Although Roosevelt's writings are not given much attention, his spirit pervades Kazin's analysis.

LORANT, STEFAN. *The Life and Times of Theodore Roosevelt.* Garden
City: Doubleday Company, Inc., 1959. Profusely illustrated; the
best of its kind in depicting the life and times of Roosevelt
through pictures and text.

MATTHEWS, BRANDER. *The Tocsin of Revolt.* New York: Charles
Scribner's Sons, 1922. Contains Matthews's evaluation of Roosevelt as a man of letters.

NYE, RUSSEL B. "Theodore Roosevelt as an Historian." *Nassau County
Historical Journal* 3:1 (1940): 3–7. This historiographical study
of Roosevelt's histories places him correctly between the patricians
and the scientific historians, and discusses his style.

POLLARD, JAMES E. *The Presidents and the Press.* New York: The
Macmillan Company, 1947. Explains Roosevelt's relationship with
the press and their indebtedness to him.

SCOTT, JAMES BROWN. "Alexander Hamilton," in *Great American
Lawyers.* Ed. William Draper Lewis. Philadelphia: The John C.
Winston Company, 1907. Excellent examination of a man who
probably had the greatest impact on Roosevelt's intellectual
development.

SMITH, EDWARD GARSTIN. *The Real Roosevelt.* Chicago: Edward
Garstin Smith Publication Company, 1910. A representative
example of the rambling, vituperative attacks which Roosevelt
suffered during his political career and which often influenced the
reviews of his books.

SULLIVAN, MARK. *Our Times, 1900–1925.* 6 vols. New York: Charles
Scribner's Sons, 1926–35. These volumes give a highly entertaining presentation of the cultural life of the United States during
Roosevelt's presidency and fairly demonstrate, with good feeling,
his effect on the country.

TRENT, W. P. "Theodore Roosevelt as a Historian." *Forum* 21 (1896):
566–76. Review; lauds Roosevelt's philosophy of history and his
open-mindedness but suggests that *The Winning of the West* is
too long.

WESTCOTT, ALLAN F. "Mr. Roosevelt as Critic." *New York Times
Literary Section,* June 12, 1910, pp. 3, 19. Examines some of
Roosevelt's reviews in *Atlantic Monthly* and elsewhere.

Index